LACenter
BV
4501.2
.S893
1983
6.95
248.4
S978d

Proven Word books have proven themselves where it counts — among the thousands of readers who have made them best-sellers because they found them meaningful in the arena of life.

These books were best-sellers in hardcover and are now offered at a more affordable price in deluxe paperback bindings.

These special editions also offer you a built-in study guide with insightful questions which will encourage group discussions as well as personal reflection and thought.

The Proven Word series answers the widespread needs of people everywhere who are searching for the answers to the pressures and problems of living in today's modern world.

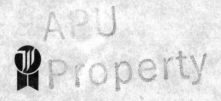
No Longer
APU
Property

MARSHBURN MEMORIAL LIBRARY
AZUSA PACIFIC UNIVERSITY
AZUSA, CALIFORNIA 91702

Dropping Your Guard

Books by Charles R. Swindoll:

Come Before Winter
Compassion: Showing Care in a Careless World
Dropping Your Guard
Encourage Me
For Those Who Hurt
Growing Deep in the Christian Life
Growing Strong in the Seasons of Life
Growing Wise in Family Life
Hand Me Another Brick
Improving Your Serve
Killing Giants, Pulling Thorns
Leadership: Influence That Inspires
Living Above the Level of Mediocrity
Living Beyond the Daily Grind I, II
Living on the Ragged Edge
Make Up Your Mind
The Quest for Character
Recovery: When Healing Takes Time
Standing Out
Starting Over
Strengthening Your Grip
Strike the Original Match
Three Steps Forward, Two Steps Back
Victory: A Winning Game Plan for Life
You and Your Child

Booklets by Charles R. Swindoll:

Anger
Attitudes
Commitment
Dealing with Defiance
Demonism
Destiny
Divorce
Eternal Security
God's Will
Hope
Impossibilities
Integrity
Leisure
The Lonely Whine of the Top Dog
Moral Purity
Our Mediator
Peace in Spite of Panic
Prayer
Sensuality
Singleness
Stress
Tongues
When Your Comfort Zone Gets the Squeeze
Woman

Charles R. Swindoll

Dropping Your Guard

WORD PUBLISHING
Dallas·London·Vancouver·Melbourne

ALDERSGATE COLLEGE
LIBRARY MARSHBURN MEMORIAL LIBRARY
AZUSA PACIFIC UNIVERSITY
AZUSA, CALIFORNIA 91702

DROPPING YOUR GUARD: THE VALUE OF OPEN RELATIONSHIPS

Copyright ©1983 by Charles R. Swindoll
Printed in the United States of America

All rights reserved. No portion of this book may be reproduced in any form except for brief quotations in reviews, without the written permission of the publisher.

Unless otherwise indicated, Scripture quotations are from *The New American Standard Bible,* copyright ©1960, 1962, 1963, 1968, 1971, 1972, 1973, 1975, 1977 by the Lockman Foundation and used by permission.

Scripture quotations identified PHILLIPS are from *The New Testament in Modern English*, copyright ©1958, 1960, 1972 by J. B. Phillips.

Scripture quotations identified NIV are from the Holy Bible: New International Version, copyright ©1978 by the New York International Bible Society. Used by permission of Zondervan Bible Publishers.

Scripture quotations identified NKJV are from the New King James Version. Copyright ©1979, 1980, 1982 by Thomas Nelson, Inc., Publishers.

Scripture quotations identified TEV are from the *Good News Bible,* the Bible in Today's English Version, copyright ©American Bible Society 1976.

Library of Congress Cataloging in Publication Data

Swindoll, Charles R.
Dropping your guard.

1. Christian life — 1960 –   2. Interpersonal
relations.   I. Title.
BV4501.2.S893   1983   248.4   83-17021
ISBN 0–8499–0352–1 (regular edition)
ISBN 0–8499–3850–3 (delux edition)
ISBN 0–8499–3213–0 (paperback edition)

2 3 4 5 6 7 8 9 LBM 7 6 5 4

DEDICATION

Several years ago I made an extremely important decision.

Finding myself pushed and pressured from a dozen different sources, I realized the need to pull up close to a small group of men—objective men, trustworthy men—tough-minded and insightful enough to see things I could not see, yet honest enough to tell me the truth and caring enough to encourage me. Integrity, confidentiality, availability, humility, and a consistent, sensitive walk with the Lord were essential traits each man needed to model.

Now that God has led us together and some stability has returned to my life (as well as my sanity), I realize the value of being surrounded by and accountable to such a wholesome body of counselors. They have become my closest friends. I am grateful for the hours they have willingly invested on my behalf. The nature of our relationship requires that they remain anonymous . . . but God, who will reward openly all efforts expended for Him in secret, will one day unload the truck of His heavenly riches and crown them with many crowns.

To these faithful friends, who have taught me so much about dropping my guard and who have given me the freedom to be completely myself, I dedicate the pages and the principles of this book.

Contents

Introduction   9

1. Loosening the Mask: How It All Began   15
2. Digging Deeper, Risking Change   28
3. Getting Closer, Growing Stronger   46
4. Operation Assimilation   62
5. United and Invincible   79
6. When the Fellowship Breaks Down   97
7. Authentic Love   114
8. Needed: Shelter for Storm Victims   127
9. Some Things Have Gotta Go!   143
10. Choose for Yourself   156
11. The Necessity of Accountability   168
12. A Hope Transplant: The Essential Operation   187
Conclusion   205
Notes   208

Introduction

"Okay, everybody, *masks off!*"

There are times I want to stand up and make that announcement. I've never done it, you understand, but I sure have been tempted. Can you imagine the reaction?

It would be a scary thing for most folks, especially those who have learned that survival comes a lot easier behind a mask. There's a mask for whatever the occasion—have you noticed? No matter how you really feel, regardless of the truth, if you become skilled at hiding behind your guard, you don't have to hassle all the things that come with full disclosure. You feel safe. What you lack in honesty, you make up for in pseudo-security.

If you wear an "I'm tough" mask, you don't have to worry about admitting how weak and frightened you actually are. If you keep your "I'm holy" mask in place, you never need to bother with people wondering if you struggle with spirituality. Furthermore, the "I'm-cool-because-I've-got-it-all-together" mask comes in handy if you resist stuff like hard questions, vulnerable admissions, straight talk. Another familiar front is the "I'm-able-to-handle-all-this-pain-and-pressure" mask. No tears, not even a frown or hint of bewilderment is revealed. That one helps when you're surrounded by superpious folks who are impressed with answers like, "Oh, I'm fine" and "I'm just claiming the victory," accompanied by eyelids at half mast and a nice, appropriate smile. There are even "intellectual-and-scholarly" masks that protect you from having to face the practical nitty-gritty.

There is just one major difficulty in this mask-wearing game—*it isn't real.* It therefore forces us to skate rather than relate. It promotes a phony-baloney, make-a-good-impression attitude instead of an honest realism that relieves and frees. What's worse, as we hide the truth behind a veneer polished to a high gloss, we become lonely instead of understood and loved for who we are. And the most tragic part of all is that the longer we do it, the better we get at it . . . and the more alone we remain in our hidden world of fear, pain, anger, insecurity, and grief—all those normal and natural emotions we hesitate to admit but that prove we are only human.

The result? Distance. Distance that makes you out of focus with me—removed from me by closed-off compartments that stay locked, keeping us from being able to know each other and, when and where necessary, to help each other. But the fact remains that distance must be removed if we hope to cope in this generation of excessive individualism. We need each other! All the uncertainty notwithstanding, the rewards of dropping your guard will far outweigh the risks involved. But the problem is how to convince you that it is worth the effort, especially if you have become adept at using masks . . . and who hasn't?

This, in a single statement, is my objective in writing this book: I would like to convince you of the value of open relationships. Perhaps you wonder why I want to do that, since you and I don't know each other. Why would I write a book like this? How could it help you?

I can think of two reasons. First, because I, personally, lived too many of my years with my guard up. I will never forget the consequences, nor would I if I could. Living a closed life, trying to play a part that wasn't me led to nothing but greater fear and higher defenses. I want to identify with where you are and help you know there's a better way to spend the rest of your life. I care too much to let you go on thinking you're stuck with that mask from now on.

Second, because I now know the joy and freedom of having my guard down, I no longer feel any need to fool anybody, to play the mask game, to make verbal sounds with my mouth that my mind knows aren't true. I want you to make the same discovery. And what a great way to live!

"Is it really *that* different?" you ask. It's the difference between a slow fuzzy worm and a lacy butterfly . . . between being bound up in some dark corner questioning your own worth, hoping people won't find out how human you really are, and being free to let the truth be known . . . to hide no longer . . . to be confident and secure while you remain one hundred percent human, without any mask of hypocrisy. I want to help you start your journey down that road.

The purpose of the journey, of course, is not simply to unmask and parade our pain as we expose the truth of who we are. That's merely the means to an end. The *ultimate* objective is to cultivate an atmosphere of such openness that we are free to share our dreams in an unguarded manner, talk about hopes, and hammer out our goals in life. By becoming people who are comfortable to be around, we encourage the same in others. In the process, a grinding existence changes into meaningful living as we replace our isolationism with involvement in the lives of others.

Let me assure you of something lest you assume the wrong thing. This book is not based on some humanistic philosophy or pop psychology or ego-centered mentality. I should tell you up front, I am one who believes completely in the Bible. As a minister by profession, I have been absorbing the teachings of Scripture every year of my adult life since the late 1950s, and I have been communicating those principles every week, often several times a week, since that time. The lens through which I filter my perceptions and my convictions is, therefore, the Bible. Its relevance and its wisdom will be seen as each chapter of this book develops. Hopefully, you will discover that God's Word is both timely and true, able to release you from the thick cocoon of fear and give you wings to fly free of all masks. Contrary to popular opinion, God gave us His Book to release us to reach our full potential . . . not to push us into a corner and watch us squirm!

I am indebted to my secretary, Helen Peters, for her tireless and patient efforts as she has happily typed and retyped the manuscript. All authors should have such superb assistance! My friends at Word Books also deserve a round of applause for their incessant commitment to me and to a quality product: "Doc" Heatherley, Floyd Thatcher, Ernie Owen, Bob Wolgemuth, and my careful editor with an eye for detail, Beverly Phillips. Each one has played a valuable part in seeing this volume reach completion.

I appreciate the artistic skills of my long-time friend, Paul Lewis, who created the cover idea and design . . . and also my thanks to Jim Killion for helping me choose the title.

I also declare my gratitude to the congregation I have had the privilege of serving as senior pastor since 1971, the First Evangelical Free Church of Fullerton, California. With contagious enthusiasm, this faithful flock packs the house Sunday after Sunday to worship and to respond to the truths of God's Word, the Bible. Originally, the thoughts that have now found their way into these chapters were sermons I preached. Because of the positive reaction of so many who first heard those sermons and encouraged me to publish the insights God showed me and allowed me to share, the book is now a reality.

Finally, I wish to thank my wife and family for understanding how much I love to write and how much time and effort such an undertaking demands. Had they not surrounded me with the freedom, affirmation, and encouragement to stay at the task, *Dropping Your Guard* would have been renamed *Losing Your Mind.*

CHARLES R. SWINDOLL
Fullerton, California

1

Loosening the Mask:
How It All Began

ANNIVERSARIES ARE GREAT occasions for evaluation. Once we get beyond the nostalgia and choke back a few tears, it's amazing how objective we can become. Hindsight has a lot of insight.

A couple of years ago I completed ten years of ministry at the church I serve in Fullerton, California. We don't make big deals out of anniversaries (I'm happy to say), but it was a good time to appraise where we had been. We have gone through the common cycle familiar to growing churches: solid beginning, steady growth, expansion on the original site, greater growth, multiple services (ultimately *five* services a Sunday for almost four years!), plans for relocation, purchase of larger site, construction phase, and final move followed by dedication of the new facilities. Whew! Makes me weary just writing all that down. Each part of the cycle carried with it its own set of problems and delights.

As I reflected on the previous decade that Sunday afternoon

following the brief anniversary commemoration, I had several flashes of insight. Strong were my feelings of gratitude both to God and to the Fullerton flock. How flexible those people had been . . . how forgiving . . . how supportive and enthusiastic! Through all the changes and cramped conditions and parking problems and crowded hallways and financial crises and personal demands, they hung in there. Even though we looked more like Disneyland than a church (especially to our neighbors on the outside), we maintained our sanity and our unity within, and we finally were able to settle down and get back to the business of ministry. There was only one problem—*we were full again!* We were having to turn people away. And I should add that our parking lot was woefully inadequate. It had all the signs of the old "same-song-second-verse" syndrome.

Rethinking Growth

There are times when a leader is forced to face some very painful facts. That afternoon I began to do that. I realized that growth can be measured in more ways than numerically. There is something significantly more important than growing larger. Even though it is the most popular way to determine "success," more isn't necessarily better. In spite of all the excitement that goes along with rapid growth and crowded conditions, there are some drawbacks. It is easy to be lost and feel lonely in a crowd—even at a place of worship. People begin to look the same. Names start running together and before long seem less important. Needs are bypassed. The main concerns seem to be finding a parking space and getting a seat. If we're not careful, we begin to resemble a school of voracious piranha instead of a tender flock of sheep. Worst of all, the church becomes like the world rather than distinct from it. "Dog eat dog" is simply changed to "sheep eat sheep."

None of this is intended, you understand. No one ever stands up and blows a whistle to make everybody run like rats on a ship. And, believe me, none of this growth was orchestrated in my mind or the minds of my colleagues. I distinctly remember the first time I read that our congregation was referred to as a "super church." I felt uneasy with the label. It smacked of Madison Avenue hype, shallow and slick programming, all the stuff that I've never wanted to be identified with. But I couldn't get around it, our numerical size gave us the label. How could we solve the dilemma? Was it possible to be large in number yet deep in the things that matter? Why couldn't we have greater personal involvement along with a broader base of ministry? Can't size and depth coexist? Isn't it possible to relate to one another even though there are several thousand of us? Those questions haunted me. And even though a large number of "authorities" had attempted to answer them (many of whom said, "It can't happen"), none seemed to satisfy.

HEARING GOD'S APPRAISAL

I decided to hear what God had to say. While doing a brief survey of the growth of the early church in the book of Acts, I discovered how large a body the first century church actually was. First, three thousand; soon, a couple more thousand; and some time later, several thousand more. It was, nevertheless, a dynamic and caring group. I found myself intrigued and relieved. There was balance between taking in and giving out, between hearing and doing, between receiving instruction and being personally involved in each others' lives. I smiled as I read words like:

> And they were continually devoting themselves to the apostles' teaching and to fellowship, to the breaking of bread and to prayer.
> And everyone kept feeling a sense of awe; and many wonders and signs were taking place through the apostles.
> And all those who had believed were together, and had all things in common; and they began selling their property and possessions, and were sharing them with all, as anyone might have need. (Acts 2:42–45).

And the congregation of those who believed were of one heart and soul; and not one of them claimed that anything belonging to him was his own; but all things were common property to them.

And with great power the apostles were giving witness to the resurrection of the Lord Jesus, and abundant grace was upon them all.

For there was not a needy person among them, for all who were owners of land or houses would sell them and bring the proceeds of the sales, and lay them at the apostles' feet; and they would be distributed to each, as any had need (Acts 4:32–35).

And at the hand of the apostles many signs and wonders were taking place among the people; and they were all with one accord in Solomon's portico.

But none of the rest dared to associate with them; however, the people held them in high esteem.

And all the more believers in the Lord, multitudes of men and women, were constantly added to their number; to such an extent that they even carried the sick out into the streets, and laid them on cots and pallets, so that when Peter came by, at least his shadow might fall on any one of them.

And also the people from the cities in the vicinity of Jerusalem were coming together, bringing people who were sick or afflicted with unclean spirits; and they were all being healed (Acts 5:12–16).

Therefore, those who had been scattered went about preaching the word.

And Philip went down to the city of Samaria and began proclaiming Christ to them.

And the multitudes with one accord were giving attention to what was said by Philip, as they heard and saw the signs which he was performing.

For in the case of many who had unclean spirits, they were coming out of them shouting with a loud voice; and many who had been paralyzed and lame were healed.

And there was much rejoicing in that city (Acts 8:4–8).

Now that's what I would call dynamic enthusiasm! I mean, those folks (though large in number) were in touch with one another. They were well-instructed yet deeply involved. Even though they were surviving in a day of persecution and martyrdom, they weren't satisfied simply to come together, soak up the scoop, then hide out until the next secret meeting. I didn't find an uninvolved isolationist in the entire bunch.

While pondering that thought, I turned back to Solomon's comment regarding our need for other people:

> Two are better than one because they have a good return for their labor.
> For if either of them falls, the one will lift up his companion. But woe to the one who falls when there is not another to lift him up.
> Furthermore, if two lie down together they keep warm, but how can one be warm alone?
> And if one can overpower him who is alone, two can resist him. A cord of three strands is not quickly torn apart (Eccles. 4:9–12).

As I think back, I recall getting a pencil and making a few notes in the margin of my Bible. I thought about our congregation in light of those four verses, and I wrote down "Crucial Factors to Be Convinced of. . . ." There were three:

- Unhealthy Consequences of Isolationism
- Essential Benefits of Relationships
- Absolute Necessity of Assimilation

I closed my eyes and allowed each point to turn over and over in my head until all the sharp edges were worn smooth. I began to realize that if we were going to keep calling ourselves a church, we would have to get serious about each of those three issues. That's how it all began. Little did I realize it would someday be the basis of a book. But now that two more years have passed and we've been infected with these germ thoughts—

and a contagious excitement now marks our ministry because of it—I can hardly wait to share with you the benefits we've begun to reap.

Before I get into that, however, let me go back to those three crucial factors I listed. I want to be sure that each one is clearly understood before I build my case in the remaining chapters.

Unhealthy Consequences of Isolationism

Before anyone can ever be convinced of the value of involvement and mutuality, that person must come to terms with the consequences of isolationism. The fact is, *we need each other.* The other side of the coin is also axiomatic: Without each other, unhealthy and unhappy things happen to us. Empirical studies and psychological analyses strongly suggest that individuals cannot function effectively without deep links to others. Continuous, meaningful, and secure bonds are essential or we risk losing our humanity.

As Bernard Berelson and Gary Steiner discovered in their overview of more than one thousand social science studies: "Total isolation is virtually always an intolerable situation for the human adult—even when physical needs are provided for." [1]

We Americans are not so convinced. Independence is our watchword and "Think for Yourself" is our motto. Declaring a need is a sign of weakness, an open admission of failure and lack of character. Furthermore, we are on the move so much, who has time to share and to care? As one wife of an executive (whose corporation moved him and his family three times in a seven-year period) recently confessed, "To decrease the pain of saying 'good-by' to our neighbors, we no longer bother to say 'hello.' " It has been my observation that we Christians are not immune from this hurry-up, hassle-hustle mentality.

Do we really move that often? I was amazed to find that the average American moves about fourteen times in his lifetime. One authority states:

Americans move around more than most people, and hence find it more difficult to sustain intensive friendships and bonds among neighbors, even kinship. In an average year, some 40 million Americans move. Put another way, every ten years, between 40 and 60 percent of an average American town's population leaves.[2]

Do you realize the average worker keeps his job only 3.6 years?[3] It is no small wonder that popular sociologist Vance Packard believes:

. . . rootlessness seems clearly to be associated with a decline in companionship, a decline in satisfying group activities, a decline in mutual trust, and a decline in psychological security. It encourages a shallowness in personal relationships and a relative indifference to community problems.[4]

You and I probably don't need a great deal more literary evidence from professional journals to prove how damaging isolationism can be. Just read the backgrounds of those who climb up into towers and shoot total strangers on the street below. Or do your own investigation of twisted and sadistic murderers. How often we find that they are products of our do-your-own-thing philosophy that holds people at a distance and implies a sneering "who needs you?" This whole ego-centered mentality is being pushed to an extreme and popularized by numerous volumes that make their way to the best-seller list . . . such as *How to Be Your Own Best Friend,* in which psychologists Newman and Berkowitz assert: "We are accountable only to ourselves for what happens to us in our lives."[5]

Even though it is easy to buy into the selfish lifestyle and opt for isolationism instead of involvement, the consequences are bitter and inescapable. That's why the simple, profound counsel of Solomon remains so needed: "Two are better than one. . . ." Swimming with the current of today's me-ism mindset has a way of eclipsing the contrasting light of Scripture.

Essential Benefits of Relationships

If you will return with me to that ancient king's comment, you'll find several reasons behind his statement "Two are better than one. . . ." This is true because:

- they have a good return for their labor (v. 9)
  Mutual effort
- one will lift up his companion (v. 10)
  Mutual support
- they keep [each other] warm (v. 11)
  Mutual encouragement
- they can resist an attack (v. 12)
  Mutual strength

If ever we needed a renewal, a renewal of meaningful relationships is long overdue! I'm not suggesting we must surrender our own individuality and become submerged in the slimy swamp of group-think. Nor do I extol the virtues of mediocrity as our standard. That's not my interest or concern. What does disturb me is the mentality that implies an excessive independence.

Thinking back upon Solomon's words, it is only when I *share* life's experiences with others that I can enjoy them or endure them to the greatest advantage. This is what those early Christians did. They learned quickly that survival would go hand-in-hand with "fellowship." Unfortunately, that term has lost its punch now that it has fallen into the bag of Christian clichés. But originally, the Greek word *koinonia* conveyed the idea of sharing, having something in common with another, entering into another's life and, if needed, assisting the person. You see, having a relationship calls for being in fellowship with others, and that cannot be done very easily at arm's length. It implies getting in touch, feeling the hurts, being an instrument of encouragement and healing. Fences must come down. Masks need to come off. Welcome signs need to be hung outside the door. Keys to the locks in our lives must be duplicated and distributed.

Bridges need to be lowered that allow others to cross the moat and then share our joys and our sorrows.

Our pioneer forefathers realized the need for this.

> The Europeans who came here to settle North America found it vast and unexplored. "Self-reliant" was the watchword, and the scout, the mountain man or the pioneer, with his axe and rifle over his shoulder, became the national hero.
>
> In those early days the government gave away quarter sections of land to anyone who would homestead, in order to encourage settlement. People flocked west from crowded cities and villages to have their own land at last. Before they could farm the land they had chosen, their first job was to build a sod hut to live in, and we know that most families built them right smack-dab in the middle of their quarter section. The reason was obvious. People who had never owned land before had a new sense of pride and ownership. They wanted to feel that everything they saw belonged to them.
>
> But that custom changed very quickly. This chosen isolation did strange things to people. Occasionally, photographers went out to record life on the frontier and returned with photographs of weird men, wild-eyed women, and haunted-looking children. Before long most of these families learned to move their houses to one corner of their property in order to live in proximity with three other families who also lived on the corners of their property. Four families living together, sharing life and death, joy and sorrow, abundance and want, had a good chance of making it.[6]

In our local church, when this whole idea moved from theory to tangible reality, we decided to stop treating our single parents like second-class citizens. We announced the formation of *Single Parents Fellowship* (notice that last word), and we invited them to come together. Hundreds emerged from our congregation. Some were frightened and hurting. Some were reluctant, insecure, and suspicious. Some were angry, others anxious. But out they came. And what a "fellowship" it has become! Since then we have encouraged those who have struggled with drug abuse and alcoholism to drop their guard, come out of the closet, and meet with others who have similar battles. Although naturally more reluctant than our SPF group to begin with, they now meet each week—over fifty brave, vulnerable men and women—to share their pain and to enter into a meaningful relationship with one another.

As I mentioned in one of my films,[7] the group wanted to have a name (certainly something other than "All Those Who Struggle with Booze and Dope"!), so they carried out an intense search through the Scriptures. When they came upon 1 Peter 5:8, they found their name—*Lion Tamers Anonymous.* Remember the verse? "Be sober, be vigilant; because your adversary the devil walks about like a roaring lion, seeking whom he may devour" (NKJV). What a great group of unmasked souls . . . and what honesty when they meet and relate!

And next, in light of the economic crunch that has struck our country in the early 1980s, we have established a fellowship group for the unemployed—*Breadwinners in Transition.* We have developed ways to encourage these often-depressed individuals, giving serious thought to how we might preserve their dignity and uphold their self-esteem. Along with providing regular meetings, we have several of our laymen and laywomen helping them find employment. Containers for nonperishable foods are filled, distributed, and maintained by others who assist in this ministry.

We have also opened our arms to the parents of the brain-damaged, the mentally retarded in our church and community. We call this once-a-month group meeting PEP—*Parents of Exceptional People.* One of their activities is a Special Olympics program. And on a Saturday afternoon not long ago, many of us gathered to encourage these marvelous people who were participating in this program. It took one youngster in a wheelchair about twenty minutes to finish the fifty-yard dash, but young and old alike were on the sidelines cheering her on.

I could easily fill another page or two describing how we are learning to relate to our many senior citizens with a group called *Forever Young.* We also have a group for those who are left with the responsibility of caring for their dependent parents. This group is called CODA—*Children of Dependent Adults.*

The benefits of relating brought about by these groups seems limitless.

ABSOLUTE NECESSITY OF ASSIMILATION

We've considered the consequences of isolationism and the benefits of relationships. You probably agree with both, but your question is "How?" How can a large church that attracts so many people from such varied backgrounds harness the energy and move people from mere spectators to participants? I can assure you it doesn't happen automatically. People don't suddenly get involved, drop their guard, and devote themselves to one another. The secret is a firm commitment to assimilation.

As I realized how easily our church could become a huge body of spectators, strangers to one another and rootless in our commitment to Christ, I began to speak on the value of becoming involved in a small-group ministry—an adult-fellowship group, a choir, an evangelistic team, a prayer group, a weekly home Bible class, one of our women's organizations or men's groups. In any one of these special groups, there could be more in-depth sharing and involvement. I began digging into the Scriptures to find out all I could from God's Word. To my amazement, there was a massive amount of biblical material supporting the concept of assimilation. In fact, the balance of this book is a compilation of my findings. And it is my hope that each one who reads these pages will realize the necessity of being more than a Sunday spectator, rather a consistent participant in the things of God.

Perhaps it would help, as I close this chapter, if I gave you a working definition of *assimilation*. When I use that term I have in mind *becoming absorbed in the function of the Body of Christ as an active participant, relating to, sharing with, and caring for others in the Body.* Until this becomes a part of our lives, until we move out of the stands of formal religion and onto the playing field of authentic Christianity, it is extremely doubtful that our walk with God will ever reach its full potential.

Let me ask you a tough question, my friend. How serious is your interest in your spiritual growth? If you are satisfied to skate along, pushed by this gust of wind and attracted by that shallow fad, then you'll not have much interest in the pages that follow. In fact, if you've decided not to let Christ get much beyond the front door of your heart, you may feel that I'm getting into areas that are none of my business. But if you are sincerely hungry for maturity—if you are sick and tired of being a spectator and you long to let Christ invade every room of your life, rearranging the furniture of your mind and getting control of the appetites of your heart—you are obviously ready to dig deeper.

DISCUSSION IDEAS AND QUESTIONS

- In your own words, state the main idea of chapter 1, using a sentence or two.
- Do you agree or disagree? Discuss why.
- Can you remember the three crucial factors that were developed in the last half of the chapter? Try to name them.
- Choose one of the three and talk about some actual cases you are aware of in your neighborhood, your church, or where you work. In other words, can you think of an individual or group of individuals who fit into one of those three categories?
- Turn back to the references from the book of Acts. Read each passage aloud and slowly. Discuss the thing(s) that stand out most significantly to you as you picture those early Christians in your mind.
- Read Ecclesiastes 4:9–12. Share a particular occasion in your own life where you benefited from having someone alongside as you went through a specific need.
- Pause and pray. Give God thanks for someone who helped you at a hard time in your past.
- Before leaving, find someone in your group to thank for something he/she has done for you. Try to express to that individual what he/she has meant to you.

2

Digging Deeper,
Risking Change

It is the nature of the beast within all of us to resist change. The familiar draws us in and constrains us like a magnet. Most folks would rather stay the same and suffer than risk change and find relief. This is especially true when the future seems threatening. Being creatures of habit, many would much rather frown at today's familiar misery and stay in the mess than smile at tomorrow's unsure adventure.

If I don't miss my guess, you drive to work the same way day after day. Unless you are among the few who fight routine, it probably doesn't interest you to consider a new route. And how about your approach to solving problems? If you're like most, it's doubtful that creativity plays a big role in that process either. The strangest part of all is this: Even when we know ever so clearly that it is God who is leading us away from the familiar and into a new adventure, we break out in a rash.

How often I have seen this in couples who fall in love and make plans for marriage. God brings them together, strengthens their relationship, and convinces them they should leave the single life behind and go for it. Farewell to studio apartments and loneliness; good-by skydiving, no insurance, tiny sports cars, and tables set for one. Long live joint-checking accounts and double beds and bicycles built for two and new babies and station wagons! But something weird happens when ye olde wedding day arrives. We're talking cold, sweaty palms and feelings of doubt, maybe sheer panic. Why? It's the "What in the world am I doing?" syndrome—the familiar versus the unfamiliar wrestling match.

Church congregations can go through the same mental crunch. For a period of time things stay pretty much the same. Everybody knows everybody. All is quiet on the stained-glass front. Things are little and manageable and predictable. Friends and families remain close, intimacy flows naturally. Then God steps in and shakes things up. New faces; rapid growth; increased staff; adjustments; less than comfortable surroundings; additional services to meet the demand; loss of the laid-back, relaxed style of yesteryear . . . and there it is again—resistance, reluctance to change. As Cervantes says in *Don Quixote*, we long to "return to our flesh pots of Egypt."

That's not an original thought with Cervantes, you know. He lifted it from the biblical account of the ancient Hebrews when they left Egypt under Moses' leadership. What a story! I'd like us to think about it for awhile.

The Exodus was not only remarkable, it was the next thing to a miracle. God broke the yoke of over four hundred years of slavery, mistreatment, and all manner of indignity. He promised them a new land—one they could call their own. But, like the ship's crew on Columbus's maiden voyage across the Atlantic, mutiny soon replaced unity.

Get a load of this:

"Why did we ever leave Egypt?" (Num. 11:20).

And a little later:

> Then all the congregation lifted up their voices and cried, and the people wept that night.
>
> And all the sons of Israel grumbled against Moses and Aaron; and the whole congregation said to them, "Would that we had died in the land of Egypt! Or would that we had died in this wilderness!
>
> "And why is the Lord bringing us into this land, to fall by the sword? Our wives and our little ones will become plunder; would it not be better for us to return to Egypt?"
>
> So they said to one another, "Let us appoint a leader and return to Egypt" (Num. 14:1–4).

Who said that? A bunch of ill-treated, forgotten wanderers who had been abandoned and left to die? No way! Those are the words of folks who had been delivered from bondage, miraculously protected, divinely fed, and securely led—the people of the Exodus. And yet they are begging to return, pleading for those "flesh pots of Egypt." Why?

Tests That Tempt Us to Retreat

Under Moses' direction the Jews escaped from Pharaoh's rule. Obviously, it was the Lord God who made this possible, as Moses himself declared.

> And Moses said to the people, "Remember this day in which you went out from Egypt, from the house of slavery; for by a powerful hand the Lord brought you out from this place. And nothing leavened shall be eaten.
>
> "On this day in the month of Abib, you are about to go forth.
>
> "And it shall be when the Lord brings you to the land of the Canaanite, the Hittite, the Amorite, the Hivite and the Jebusite, which He swore to your fathers to give you, a land flowing with milk and honey, that you shall observe this rite in this month" (Exod. 13:3–5).

Their destination? He called it "a land flowing with milk and honey"—the country of Canaan. God assured them that He would see them through *regardless*. Little did they realize, however, the way He would accomplish that objective. That's where things got sticky. They were going to be challenged and stretched like never before in their lives. The predictable, business-as-usual routine they and their fathers before them had known was about to be disrupted by a series of tests—tests designed by God to force them to drop their defensive and traditional guard and trust Him! I find five such tests: unfamiliar surprises, unwanted fears, unpleasant adversaries, unfair accusations, unexpected resistance.

Unfamiliar Surprises

Read the following rather carefully.

> Now it came about when Pharaoh had let the people go, that God did not lead them by the way of the land of the Philistines, even though it was near; for God said, "Lest the people change their minds when they see war, and they return to Egypt."
>
> Hence God led the people around by the way of the wilderness to the Red Sea; and the sons of Israel went up in martial array from the land of Egypt.
>
> And Moses took the bones of Joseph with him, for he had made the sons of Israel solemnly swear, saying, "God shall surely take care of you; and you shall carry my bones from here with you."
>
> Then they set out from Succoth and camped in Etham on the edge of the wilderness.
>
> And the Lord was going before them in a pillar of cloud by day to lead them on the way, and in a pillar of fire by night to give them light, that they might travel by day and by night.
>
> He did not take away the pillar of cloud by day, nor the pillar of fire by night, from before the people (Exod. 13:17–22).

You can't appreciate the full meaning of these words without a map of that ancient region. Suffice it to say, the most logical journey would have been "by the way of the land of the Philistines." It was nearer and less arduous. The other route was farther, less comfortable, more threatening, and included a dead end at the Red Sea. But since when did human logic dictate to divine leading?

By the way, are you going through a few surprises these days? Are you being led away from familiar turf and into a "wilderness" journey? There's nothing to fear so long as you know God is in it. He's good at surprises, you know.

Unwanted Fears

They got as far as the sea. Naturally, they were forced to stop and wait for the next move. The scene was frightening.

> Then the Egyptians chased after them with all the horses and chariots of Pharaoh, his horsemen and his army, and they overtook them camping by the sea, beside Pi-hahiroth, in front of Baalzephon.
> And as Pharaoh drew near, the sons of Israel looked, and behold, the Egyptians were marching after them, and they became very frightened; so the sons of Israel cried out to the Lord.
> Then they said to Moses, "Is it because there were no graves in Egypt that you have taken us away to die in the wilderness? Why have you dealt with us in this way, bringing us out of Egypt?
> "Is this not the word that we spoke to you in Egypt, saying, 'Leave us alone that we may serve the Egyptians'? For it would have been better for us to serve the Egyptians than to die in the wilderness" (Exod. 14:9–12).

Remember, these are people who have above their heads a visible cloud assuring them of God's presence *and* still ringing in their ears is God's promise of protection—Canaan would be theirs to claim. But it's astounding how fear can silence all that. Behind them was an army of Egyptians, south of them was a desert, north of them was a range of mountains, and immediately in front of them was a large, wet, intimidating body of water. Enter: fear. Exit: faith. So Moses spoke to the issue.

But Moses said to the people, "Do not fear! Stand by and see the salvation of the Lord which He will accomplish for you today; for the Egyptians whom you have seen today, you will never see them again forever.

"The Lord will fight for you while you keep silent." Then the Lord said to Moses, "Why are you crying out to me? Tell the sons of Israel to go forward.

"And as for you, lift up your staff and stretch out your hand over the sea and divide it, and the sons of Israel shall go through the midst of the sea on dry land.

"And as for Me, behold, I will harden the hearts of the Egyptians so that they will go in after them; and I will be honored through Pharaoh and all his army, through his chariots and his horsemen.

"Then the Egyptians will know that I am the Lord, when I am honored through Pharaoh, through his chariots and his horsemen" (Exod. 14:13–18).

Then Moses stretched out his hand over the sea; and the Lord swept the sea back by a strong east wind all night, and turned the sea into dry land, so the waters were divided.

And the sons of Israel went through the midst of the sea on the dry land, and the waters were like a wall to them on their right hand and on their left (Exod. 14:21–22).

And that's *exactly* what occurred. To top it off, once the Hebrews got across the sea, God took care of any further worry they might have concerning the Egyptians.

Then the Lord said to Moses, "Stretch out your hand over the sea so that the waters may come back over the Egyptians, over their chariots and their horsemen."

So Moses stretched out his hand over the sea, and the sea returned to its normal state at daybreak, while the Egyptians were fleeing right into it; then the Lord overthrew the Egyptians in the midst of the sea.

And the waters returned and covered the chariots and the horsemen, even Pharaoh's entire army that had gone into the sea after them; not even one of them remained (Exod. 14:26–28).

I'd call that covering all the bases. Wonder what the Hebrews thought as they watched an unexpected Plan B take place before their eyes. Did they learn a permanent lesson? Hardly.

Unpleasant Adversities

A little later, as they were getting closer to their destination and weary from their long trip, the Hebrews did what came naturally. They started longing for the familiar.

> Now the people became like those who complain of adversity in the hearing of the Lord; and when the Lord heard it, His anger was kindled, and the fire of the Lord burned among them and consumed some of the outskirts of the camp.
>
> The people therefore cried out to Moses, and Moses prayed to the Lord, and the fire died out.
>
> So the name of that place was called Taberah, because the fire of the Lord burned among them.
>
> And the rabble who were among them had greedy desires; and also the sons of Israel wept again, and said, "Who will give us meat to eat?
>
> "We remember the fish which we used to eat free in Egypt, the cucumbers and the melons and the leeks and the onions and the garlic, but now our appetite is gone. There is nothing at all to look at except this manna" (Num. 11:1–6).

You see, it takes a heavenly appetite to enjoy a heavenly food. Back in Egypt they wanted relief—but they wanted it on *their terms.* They desired to break free from slavery, but there wasn't any reason for everything to be taken away! They longed for the familiar and satisfying surroundings of the fertile Nile valley. After all, there was a nice variety of things to eat back in Egypt— fish, fresh stuff for salads, a few spices. But now? Warm water from a rock and manna. Every day . . . manna. They boiled it, baked it, sliced it, fixed it in pies. You name it, they tried it. I can see it now:

Mrs. Moses' 1001 Ways to Fix Manna was a bestseller. When they heard the dinner bell, nobody asked, "What's for supper?"

but rather, "How'd you fix it this time?" And that was getting old. Egypt was looking better to these weary travelers with each step they took and Canaan was fast losing its luster.

Unfair Accusations

Add to all this the burdens of leading a thankless crowd like those Hebrews, and you can understand the following:

> But two men had remained in the camp; the name of one was Eldad and the name of the other Medad. And the Spirit rested upon them (now they were among those who had been registered, but had not gone out to the tent), and they prophesied in the camp.
>
> So a young man ran and told Moses and said, "Eldad and Medad are prophesying in the camp."
>
> Then Joshua the son of Nun, the attendant of Moses from his youth, answered and said, "Moses, my lord, restrain them."
>
> But Moses said to him, "Are you jealous for my sake? Would that all the Lord's people were prophets, that the Lord would put His Spirit upon them!"
>
> Then Moses returned to the camp, both he and the elders of Israel (Num. 11:26–30).

> Then Miriam and Aaron spoke against Moses because of the Cushite woman whom he had married (for he had married a Cushite woman); and they said, "Has the Lord indeed spoken only through Moses? Has He not spoken through us as well?" And the Lord heard it (Num. 12:1–2).

How unfair to strike out against the leader at a time like this! But they did. It still happens. Anyone who has been in leadership for even a little while knows the pain of being verbally assaulted. You're either king o' the hill or (more often) the bull's eye on people's dartboard.

I remember the words of Sonny Jurgensen when he was quarterback of the Washington Redskins professional football team.

He was being attacked by fan and sportswriter alike as his team was in a slump. Somebody asked him if all that flack was getting to him. He flashed a big toothless grin and replied, "Naw, not me. I've been in this game long enough to know that every week the quarterback is in either the penthouse or the outhouse!" The penthouse is a lot more fun, but a leader isn't in it nearly as much as the outhouse. And when those accusations start penetrating, we're tempted to pull out the map and retreat.

Unexpected Resistance

By the time they got to the edge of the promised land, Canaan, a final shoe hit the floor.

> Then the Lord spoke to Moses saying, "Send out for yourself men so that they may spy out the land of Canaan, which I am going to give to the sons of Israel; you shall send a man from each of their fathers' tribes, every one a leader among them."
>
> So Moses sent them from the wilderness of Paran at the command of the Lord, all of them men who were heads of the sons of Israel.
>
> So they went up and spied out the land from the wilderness of Zin as far as Rehob, at Lebo-hamath.
>
> When they had gone up into the Negev, they came to Hebron where Ahiman, Sheshai and Talmai, the descendants of Anak were. (Now Hebron was built seven years before Zoan in Egypt.)
>
> Then they came to the valley of Eshcol and from there cut down a branch with a single cluster of grapes; and they carried it on a pole between two men, with some of the pomegranates and the figs. When they returned from spying out the land, at the end of forty days, they proceeded to come to Moses and Aaron and to all the congregation of the sons of Israel in the wilderness of Paran, at Kadesh; and they brought back word to them and to all the congregation and showed them the fruit of the land.
>
> Thus they told him, and said, "We went in to the land where you sent us; and it certainly does flow with milk and honey, and this is its fruit" (Num. 13:1–3, 21–23, 25–27).

They not only had made it, they had it made. The spies stood there with undeniable evidence. Beautiful fruit . . . and not one Medfly in the country! Fabulous soil, bumper crops, plenty of water—it must have seemed unreal.

If only the story ended here and "they lived happily ever after." It doesn't. There is a big NEVERTHELESS of unbelief.

> "Nevertheless, the people who live in the land are strong, and the cities are fortified and very large; and moreover, we saw the descendants of Anak there.
>
> "Amalek is living in the land of the Negev and the Hittites and the Jebusites and the Amorites are living in the hill country, and the Canaanites are living by the sea and by the side of the Jordan."
>
> Then Caleb quieted the people before Moses, and said, "We should by all means go up and take possession of it, for we shall surely overcome it."
>
> But the men who had gone up with him said, "We are not able to go up against the people, for they are too strong for us."
>
> So they gave out to the sons of Israel a bad report of the land which they had spied out, saying, "The land through which we have gone, in spying it out, is a land that devours its inhabitants; and all the people whom we saw in it are men of great size.
>
> "There also we saw the Nephilim (the sons of Anak are part of the Nephilim); and we became like grasshoppers in our own sight, and so we were in their sight" (Num. 13:28–33).

"Oh, no! Not giants! Not *another* problem on top of all we've had to face. Not that!" Have you felt like that lately? Have you been hearing the footsteps of giants? Or have you run into the belly of some unexpected giant that has lumbered across the landscape of your life?

I distinctly recall an evening I went to the Los Angeles Forum to watch the Los Angeles Lakers play the Philadelphia '76ers. A friend of mine had season tickets right down on the floor, just behind the Laker bench. Talk about feeling insignificant! Those guys are big even when they are sitting down. Then when they unfolded those legs and stood to full height, it was Operation Grasshopper in our section! I fully expected Abdul-Jabbar or Moses Malone to bring rain. You can't appreciate how massive those giants are until you have them within arm's reach. It's enough to make a grown man run and hide.

While I understand the spies' feeling intimidated, I cannot excuse their forgetting God's unconditional promise. Furthermore, no giant is any match for God. When God stands, everybody is smaller. When God promises, nobody dares to question it.

BARRIERS THAT KEEP US FROM RETURNING

"How does all this relate to me personally?" you, no doubt, are asking. It's a good question, and I commend you for thinking it.

My hope is to help you feel more and more comfortable being who you really are. Without trying to frighten you, I want to challenge you to risk a new horizon . . . to trust God to free you from your Egypt and to help you discover your Canaan. Now I should warn you, it will not be a quick 'n easy process. That's why I took so much time spelling out some of the tests you can expect to encounter. You'll have an "army" of voices out of your past hot on your trail, bound and determined to bring you back into captivity. You will face a Red Sea (perhaps *several* of them) that will appear uncrossable. And count on this, when you start getting near your objective, so near you can almost touch it, *up come the giants of resistance,* shouting, "Get out of here! You're not welcome . . . go back to where you belong! *Move!*"

How can we keep from running back? Does God say anything about what we can do to sustain the courage to keep risking? Indeed He does. All we need to do is take another look at this same Old Testament story to find those handles to grab hold of.

Let's look again at Exodus 13. That's the scene immediately following the Exodus. Fresh out of Egypt, those Hebrews had every reason to feel insecure. Why didn't they return? What was it that kept them from doing that?

Clear Direction from Above

Exodus 13:21–22 gives us the answer:

> And the Lord was going before them in a pillar of cloud by day to lead them on the way, and in a pillar of fire by night to give them light, that they might travel by day and by night.
>
> He did not take away the pillar of cloud by day, nor the pillar of fire by night, from before the people.

If Moses and those people were tempted to return, all they needed to do was look up. There it was, day after day . . . night after night. A distinct cloud covered them and led them during the daylight hours and after sundown . . . a "pillar of fire." It was no guessing game, no multifaceted Rubic's cube they had to figure out. No, God wanted them freed from Egyptian bondage.

I really don't know where you are in your pilgrimage from bondage to freedom. But I am confident of this, God will not leave you or give up on you. He wants you to know the joy of living an unmasked life. His Book, the Bible, is full of verses and principles that promise you His commitment. He won't leave you in the lurch. May I share a few of His promises with you?

> Therefore, let everyone who is godly pray to Thee in a time when Thou mayest be found; Surely in a flood of great waters they shall not reach him.
>
> Thou art my hiding place; Thou dost preserve me from trouble; Thou dost surround me with songs of deliverance.
>
> I will instruct you and teach you in the way which you should go; I will counsel you with My eye upon you (Ps. 32:6–8).
>
> Do not fear, for I am with you;
> Do not anxiously look about you, for I am your God.

I will strengthen you, surely I will help you,
Surely I will uphold you with My righteous right hand.
Behold, all those who are angered at you will be shamed and dishonored; Those who contend with you will be as nothing, and will perish.
You will seek those who quarrel with you, but will not find them, Those who war with you will be as nothing, and nonexistent.
For I am the Lord your God, who upholds your right hand, Who says to you, "Do not fear, I will help you" (Isa. 41:10–13).

Can a woman forget her nursing child, And have no compassion on the son of her womb? Even these may forget, but I will not forget you.
Behold, I have inscribed you on the palms of My hands; Your walls are continually before Me (Isa. 49:15–16).

"And you shall know the truth, and the truth shall make you free" (John 8:32).

What then shall we say to these things? If God is for us, who is against us?
He who did not spare His own Son, but delivered Him up for us all, how will He not also with Him freely give us all things?
Who will bring a charge against God's elect? God is the one who justifies; who is the one who condemns? Christ Jesus is He who died, yes, rather who was raised, who is at the right hand of God, who also intercedes for us.
Who shall separate us from the love of Christ? Shall tribulation, or distress, or persecution, or famine, or nakedness, or peril, or sword?
Just as it is written,

"FOR THY SAKE WE ARE BEING PUT TO DEATH ALL DAY LONG;
WE WERE CONSIDERED AS SHEEP TO BE SLAUGHTERED."

But in all these things we overwhelmingly conquer through Him who loved us (Rom. 8:31–37).

These are scriptural "anchors" you can claim, trusting God to stabilize you in the storm. Consider these words as *your* cloud by day and fire by night. Believe me, you will need them when the journey gets long and the giants are loud. These truths will keep you from returning to the misery of *your* Egypt.

Timely Relief from Discouragement

> The Lord therefore said to Moses, "Gather for Me seventy men from the elders of Israel, whom you know to be the elders of the people and their officers and bring them to the tent of meeting, and let them take their stand there with you.
> "Then I will come down and speak with you there, and I will take of the Spirit who is upon you, and will put Him upon them; and they shall bear the burden of the people with you, so that you shall not bear it all alone" (Num. 11:16–17).

Remember how Moses had become the target of their criticism and complaints? Well, he began to crack under the pile. . . . Like any one of us, it got too much for him. But God graciously relieved the pressure. And He still does that today.

In the case of Moses, the Lord brought alongside His servant a group of people to help shoulder the load he was carrying. In fact, *seventy* of them. Strong natural leaders tend not to delegate responsibility as they should. They often adopt the I'm-all-alone-in-this-battle mentality. Add to that the nobody-knows-or-cares exaggeration, and you've got stress personified. Soon discouragement slips in on the blind side and cuts our feet out from under us. At these weak points in our lives there is nothing like a friend—or a group of friends—to pull us out of our rapid descent.

My wife and I have learned that life can get pretty grim without some folks alongside us to add perspective amidst the pressure. On several occasions we have been grateful for a few couples with whom we have had the freedom to share the pain and thereby diffuse the discouragement. I have come to the conclusion that it is not possible to maintain an isolated, untouchable profile and carry out all that is involved in peeling off all the masks that keep us from being fully who we are. Moses, just like everybody else, *needed* others. So do we.

Internal Fortification from Threat

But then there are times when there is very little anyone else can do to assist us. Maybe you recall the occasion when a couple of men in the Israeli camp began to prophesy. Jealous for Moses' singular role of authority, Joshua urged him to "restrain" them. With calm, unthreatened confidence, greathearted Moses refused to do that. His answer reveals how secure he was: "But Moses said to him, 'Are you jealous for my sake? Would that all the Lord's people were prophets, that the Lord would put His Spirit upon them!' Then Moses returned to the camp, both he and the elders of Israel" (Num. 11:29–30).

Only the Lord can give us that kind of internal fortitude. And as you and I ask the Lord to give us that spirit, let's resist every temptation to think of ourselves or our particular style or thrust as exclusive. If someone else is doing it (and maybe doing it better than we), let's reject jealousy and replace it with applause. Competition has no place in the ranks of Christianity.

When I consider this problem of competition and how it affects our churches, I'm reminded of the story a lady mentioned to me several years ago. She and her family were traveling across the country in their recreational vehicle. As they drove through a small town in one of the midwestern states, they passed a little church with a most unusual name. To make sure they had not misread the sign, they drove around the block and read it again:

THE ORIGINAL CHURCH OF GOD, NUMBER TWO

Now there's a church with some history worth looking into. On another occasion Moses was in need of being vindicated.

It was when Miriam and Aaron criticized him. If you'll take the time to read the twelfth chapter of Numbers, you'll see that God personally intervened on His servant's behalf. There are still such occasions today when we are at a loss to defend ourselves or vindicate our integrity. At such times we are forced to rely solely on God's intervention. And although His timing is usually different from what we expect, He gets the job done beautifully.

I have a close, personal friend whose father has been a pastor for many, many years. The father was a man of faithfulness and consistency. But a tragic event occurred in the midyears of his ministry. He was falsely accused of adultery by the vicious tongues of several gossips. The man, though completely innocent, became the object of scandalous words which followed him like his own shadow for years. There was nothing he could say or do to vindicate himself. His son, my friend, watched during his young adult years as the unfounded lies took their toll on the lives of his parents. With silent heroism they continued to serve, trusting God to confound the critic and, in His time, vindicate the minister.

Finally, it happened. It had taken ten long years, but early one morning, unannounced, the person responsible for the false accusations appeared on the doorstep of the pastor's home. As he opened the door, he stood face-to-face with the one who had started the rumor. Tears ran down the cheeks of the critic, now broken in spirit. Pleading for forgiveness, the individual openly confessed the transgression, fully admitting guilt and blaming no one else. That person, by the way, had been under such deep conviction and turmoil that there had been no freedom to serve others or find any relief within.

Graciously and tearfully, the pastor expressed his forgiveness and assured the guilty party that there was absolutely no bitterness in his heart. He and his wife had worked their way through all that pain many years earlier. Now that he was finally vindicated, the offense had long since been diffused.

I cannot relate that story without remembering the words of Amy Carmichael:

If I say, "Yes, I forgive, but I cannot *forget*," as though the
God, who *twice* a day washes all the sands on all the shores of
all the world, could not wash such memories from my mind, then
I know nothing of Calvary love.[1]

How painful some of the days in that decade of silence must
have been for my friend's father. How hard it is to wait!

Perhaps that's where you are. The details may differ, but not
the pain. In your case, God may not have stepped in yet. Perhaps
you're still waiting, still trusting. If so, don't quit. In the meantime, here's a proverb that you might grab onto: "When a man's
ways are pleasing to the Lord, He makes even his enemies to
be at peace with him" (Prov. 16:7).

Observe that there is an absence of any reference to time
in those words. We aren't told when bitter enemies become
peaceful friends . . . only that it will occur. Hang onto that
and try your best not to be overcome by bitterness. The risk
for you is simply continuing on, regardless. It's been my observation that bitterness restrains openness. If you really desire to
drop your guard, you must first drop any lingering offense and
the bitterness it has produced.

A Penetrating Prayer

One final question needs an answer: What will keep us risking?
In other words, how can we counteract the old "Egyptian magnet" and continue pressing on into new unfamiliar territory?

If I were to put it in the form of a prayer, it would have
three simple lines, then an "Amen."

Since it's God's desire that we demonstrate a message distinct
from the insecure, fearful world around us, the first line would
be: *"Lord, intensify your distinctiveness in me."*

And since it's the uncertainty of our future that strengthens
our faith, the second would be: *"Lord, increase the risk."*

And since it's true that each one of us is to be a unique
vessel of power . . . not a faded copy, the third line would be
"Lord, enlarge the difference. Amen."

DISCUSSION IDEAS AND QUESTIONS

- Why is change so difficult, so threatening? Try to be specific in your answer.
- Can you think of a risk you took that opened a door you never dreamed possible? If you feel comfortable sharing it, please do.
- Look back into the chapter and read the five "tests" that tempt us to retreat to the familiar. Which one(s) represents a major battle in your life? Why?
- Identify with Moses for a few minutes. If you were standing in his sandals, describe how you would have felt when the criticism and grumbling began. How do you handle it when you are the target?
- Remember the passages of Scripture listed under the subheading "Clear Direction from Above"? Which one encourages you the most? Is there something that troubles you about these passages? Openly talk about the struggle.
- Finally, take a glance at the closing three-line prayer. Can you ask those things of God today? Perhaps before leaving this time of meditation, you might want to expand these three lines . . . or choose one and talk with God about it.

3

Getting Closer,
Growing Stronger

NESTLED IN THE HILLS of western Virginia is a stately old southern resort named "The Homestead"—sixteen thousand Allegheny acres of mountains, valleys, forest, deep blue sky, and clear, rippling streams. The place drips with elegance and is rich in historical significance. Washington and Jefferson strolled along those winding paths. There are few settings more suitable for gaining renewed perspective than places like this.

In the spring of 1983, I was invited by the Christian Embassy to speak at a retreat in which several Cabinet members, senators, congressmen, and high-ranking Pentagon officers and their wives were present. The Homestead was the site where we met—about fifty or more of us—to be refreshed and encouraged. Those in attendance were Christians, but the lines on their faces revealed the marks of pressure, loneliness, stress, and fatigue. There they were, some of the most decisive and important people in America, setting aside a weekend to meet with the Lord, to unload their burdens, to be together as couples, hopefully to find a little relief from their pressure-cooker world. I considered it a choice privilege to be the speaker at that retreat. God's Word met many needs as these courageous and battle-weary men and women opened their lives to the truths of Scripture. The Homestead became a haven of renewed hope.

The difference between the group at the first session on Friday and the last session on Sunday was amazing. It was the same people, you understand, but those hours they spent together paid rich dividends. At first there was distance and formality. But by the time we left one another, there had emerged a beautiful blend of oneness, mutual understanding, a breakdown of defenses, and great openness. By getting closer, we grew stronger. *It was magnificent!* As beautiful as our natural surroundings were, they could not compare with the harmony, the love, and the closeness our group cultivated in three brief days.

In all my twenty-plus years of ministry, I don't believe I have ever been among a more influential (yet emotionally battered) body of believers, but even *they*, when given the opportunity to draw close to others in a context of unguarded honesty and mutual caring, responded like you can't believe. What was it? How did the magic occur? Why would over fifty high-powered, strong leaders holding some of the most enviable positions in our nation drop their guard and blend their lives together? Believe me, it wasn't the surroundings or the food or the music or the accommodations or the speaker or the weather. It was something only the Spirit of God could have done. I shall not forget that eventful weekend in May of '83. My only regret is that *you* were not present to witness it personally. Had you been, you wouldn't be satisfied simply to read about it. You'd want to *experience* it because there are few things quite as contagious as authentic, spontaneous, unguarded love in action. It cannot be legislated or manipulated. It can only be demonstrated.

Essential Ingredients

There must be certain ingredients, however. Otherwise, every time Christians met together, this same scenario would occur, and you and I know it doesn't. What are those ingredients? At this point I am somewhat reluctant to analyze and scrutinize too specifically. Like a breathtaking sunset or the sound of a pounding surf, some things defy explanation. So let me suggest three big-picture generalizations.

First, *there must be an admission of need for others.* This means that self-sufficiency and isolationism are set aside. That's hard to do in our world of superindependence. And how easily that mindset slips into the Christian ranks: "Look, I don't need others—just gimme a good sermon on Sunday, a few cassette tapes to hold me over during the week, and my privacy." To help you realize how off the wall that philosophy really is, imagine the same idea as I couch it in the terms of a hotshot, independent football player who shows up at practice and yells:

> "Hey, coach! Don't bug me with a thick playbook and all this talk about teamwork and pulling together, okay? All I need is a stadium, a big crowd, and the ball. Working with ten other guys is a hassle and learning plays is a drag. Just gimme the ball and have everybody get outa my way. I do better all alone."

Let me ask you, how long would that young athlete be around? You see, in God's sovereign plan, He arranged things so that we would do our best work as team members. To repeat what I've said all along, we need each other. Isolationism won't work.

Second, *there must be the cultivation of deeper relationships.* This takes time, effort, and a spirit of willingness. Yes, and as we saw in chapter 2, even some risk. The larger the group, the more difficult. As we just discovered when Moses attempted to lead the Hebrews to Canaan, it is easy to pick up a blame-the-leader mentality or adopt a cynical view toward God when we fail to cultivate relationships.

The thing that drew our group together so quickly at The Homestead was the similarity of circumstances. Everybody there was being shot at by critics. They were all coming out of the same stormy political scene. There was an affinity that gave everyone immediate understanding. In a context like that, relationships flourish. But it isn't so in most churches. Thus there is the need for small groups where people can begin to build bridges to one another. By the way, the leader will need to be secure and unthreatened. Pastors, for example, who must maintain tight controls and a strongly centralized ministry where events and meetings must revolve around them will not create the climate of freedom in which relationships can flourish.

Third, *there must be a firm commitment to assimilation.* This is ground we have already covered, but because it is new terminology to many of you, repetition will help establish it clearly in your mind. It isn't enough simply to admit we need others. Nor is it sufficient to say rather loosely, "Oh, yeah, knowing a few other Christians is nice." No, I'm talking about being committed to getting beneath the surface of superficial talk . . . being interested in and accountable to other believers.

The seventeenth-century John Donne was absolutely right when only seven days before his death he wrote:

> No man is an island, entire of itself; every man is a piece of the continent, a part of the main; if a clod be washed away by the sea, Europe is the less, as well as if a promontory were, as well as if a manor of thy friends or of thine own were; any man's death diminishes me, because I am involved in mankind; and therefore never send to know for whom the bell tolls; it tolls for thee.[1]

Funny thing, folks in God's family are often far more committed to the up-front leader (pastor, director, spokesperson) than to one another. But if I understand the thrust of New Testament Christianity, God never intended our earthly allegiance to be so limited. Remember those insightful words addressed to the Corinthians?

> Now the body is not one member but many. If the foot should say, "Because I am not a hand I don't belong to the body," does that alter the fact that the foot is a part of the body? Or if the ear should say, "Because I am not an eye I don't belong

to the body," does that mean that the ear really is not part of the body? After all, if the body were all one eye, for example, where would be the sense of hearing? Or, if it were all one ear, where would be the sense of smell? But God has arranged all the parts in the one body, according to his design. . . . So that the eye cannot say to the hand, "I don't need you!" nor, again, can the head say to the feet, "I don't need you!" (1 Cor. 12:14–21, PHILLIPS).

Somehow, hero-worshiping twentieth-century Christians have great difficulty believing these words. Hopefully, *you* are different. Not until we begin to see the value of *each* member of the Body (rather than just a few of the more prominent people) will we enter into this full dimension of family life. Assimilation won't happen when most in the group are busy pushing one or two up on a pedestal.

Dangers That Lurk: Be on the Alert!

These thoughts take me back to our story in the Old Testament as Moses led the Hebrews from Egypt to Canaan. There are many remarkable and relevant analogies to be found in that story. So let's return to that ancient scene and continue our investigation. I find in Deuteronomy, chapter 6, four very real dangers that apply to us today even though they have their roots in an event that transpired many centuries ago.

The Israelites are on the edge of Canaan, you'll recall. They are about to step into a country that will challenge their commitment to Jehovah God. Moses is not only concerned for their welfare, but also for the welfare of their children, once he says good-by and they move into the promised land. He wouldn't be going with them, so his words were quite intense:

"Now this is the commandment, the statutes and the judgments which the Lord your God has commanded me to teach you, that you might do them in the land where you are going over to possess it, so that you and your son and your grandson might

fear the Lord your God, to keep all His statutes and His commandments, which I command you, all the days of your life, and that
your days may be prolonged.

"O Israel, you should listen and be careful to do it, that it
may be well with you and that you may multiply greatly, just as
the Lord, the God of your fathers, has promised you, in a land
flowing with milk and honey.

"Hear, O Israel! The Lord is our God, the Lord is one!

"And you shall love the Lord your God with all your heart
and with all your soul, and with all your might" (Deut. 6:1–5).

Feel the emotion? The man is pouring out his soul. Realizing
that he would not be among them as they invaded and inhabited
Canaan, he spoke of their need to passionately love the Lord
their God . . . to listen to His voice . . . to obey His commands
. . . to serve Him with all their heart, soul, and might. This
introduces the first danger.

1. *Falling more in love with the leader than with the Lord.*
Will you observe how clearly he turned their attention away
from himself and toward the Lord. You see, Moses is dispensable
in the Canaan project. Don't misunderstand, he was exceedingly
significant in leading them from Point A (Egypt) to Point B
(edge of Canaan), but his role of importance was obviously de-
creasing. Within a matter of days, he would be gone forever
from their sight. But the Lord would be there to sustain them.
He would never leave them.

Many years ago I read a statement that has stuck in my head
ever since. I can't remember the source, but the words have
been permanently etched in my mind: "When a man of God
dies, nothing of God dies." There is no question that leaders
are used in mighty ways to shape the lives of God's people.
Where would some of us be were it not for "the shakers and
the movers" who challenged us and motivated us? But no leader,
regardless of his or her vision, gifts, or model, is indispensable
to God's overall plan. Only God is that. We are fooling ourselves
and heading for an abrupt, disillusioning fall if our love for the
leader is greater than our love and loyalty to the Lord Himself.

On top of that, God's desire to have the Body get closer and grow stronger together will be hindered if the center of affection and attention is the leader. To go back to my football example, it is teamwork that makes for a winning season and healthy intrasquad morale. Even teams that have superstar athletes frequently mention that while they appreciate and admire the star's ability, they are a team of varied talent, not a one-man operation. A difficult struggle though it may be, Christians who hope to cultivate meaningful, lasting, and deep relationships with each other must maintain the right perspective at this point. Had the Hebrews lost their focus, Joshua would have been unable to carry on when Moses stepped aside. The servant-leader Moses made Joshua's task easier by continually turning the people's allegiance away from himself and back on the Lord.

This danger of exalting the leader above the Lord is a hindrance to closeness occuring in a group because it tends to emphasize rank and positions of earthly authority above the oneness we all have in the Savior, Jesus Christ. It's His lordship that cements us together in one unified whole, placing everyone in the same role—sheep belonging to their Shepherd. But when the leader occupies a conspicuous place of prominence, the group becomes divided rather than unified and up go the defenses, on go the masks.

With rare, masterful strokes of humility, Moses instructed the people to devote themselves to the Lord their God. That brings us to danger number two.

2. *Fixing our eyes on our immediate convenience instead of our ultimate objective.* Take a look at Moses' wise counsel:

> "And these words, which I am commanding you today, shall be on your heart; and you shall teach them diligently to your sons and shall talk of them when you sit in your house and when you walk by the way and when you lie down and when you rise up.
>
> "And you shall bind them as a sign on your hand and they shall be as frontals on your forehead.
>
> "And you shall write them on the doorposts of your house and on your gates" (Deut. 6:6–9).

It is obvious they were not to sit back, relax, and "let whatever happens, happen" in the future. Not on your life. These familiar words may have become too familiar to us. Between the lines are written diligence, hard work, a solid family life, open and very natural communication. Without these things becoming a high priority, those folks would not survive. They were to give themselves to a lifestyle of mutual sharing and caring, reminding one another of the things that had held them together and kept them strong down through the years. A careful look will help you see that this wouldn't happen automatically once they got into Canaan. They were to teach, to talk, to bind, and to write this information as they got established in the promised land.

How much easier it would have been to give their attention to getting comfortable and focusing on immediate convenience instead of this ultimate objective . . . especially since they must have been weary of the wilderness. But God knew best. If they didn't *start* right, it's doubtful they would be able to sustain their distinctiveness—ever. Objectives are easily lost. They slowly erode rather than suddenly explode, have you noticed? To illustrate how this can happen, consider this actual experience one man had in the Deep South.

> When I lived in Atlanta, several years ago, I noticed in the Yellow Pages, in the listing of restaurants, an entry for a place called Church of God Grill. The peculiar name aroused my curiosity and I dialed the number. A man answered with a cheery, "Hello! Church of God Grill!" I asked how his restaurant had been given such an unusual name, and he told me: "Well, we had a little mission down here, and we started selling chicken dinners after church on Sunday to help pay the bills. Well, people liked the chicken, and we did such a good business, that eventually we cut back on the church service. After a while we just closed down the church altogether and kept on serving the chicken dinners. We kept the name we started with, and that's Church of God Grill."[2]

While we're smiling at that true story, allow me to ask you a question. What are *your* personal objectives? How about your family's objectives? Are you still on target? Maybe in the race and pace of these days you've begun to compromise and shift for the sake of convenience. It is so easy and so natural to do. That church, for example, was originally established with one clear objective—to dispense salt and display light in a community. But now it dispenses grilled cheese sandwiches, hamburgers, french fries, and cokes. Its salt is now in a little glass container on the counter. Its light is now a neon sign.

How about your church? Given to be a lighthouse, a place of hope and refuge, is it accomplishing that ultimate objective? Are hurting people really able to be at home there? Can brokenness and pain be admitted? Is there room for those who have failed rather than achieved, those who have lost rather than won, those who *don't* have it all together? Is there still a willingness to reach out and help wounded people find inner healing and the courage to go on? I'll have much more to say about this in chapter 8, but here I wanted to direct your attention toward the "lurking danger," of focusing our interests on our immediate convenience instead of our ultimate goal.

As we continue through the sixth chapter of Deuteronomy, we read:

> "Then it shall come about when the Lord your God brings you into the land which He swore to your fathers, Abraham, Isaac and Jacob, to give you, great and splendid cities which you did not build, and houses full of all good things which you did not fill, and hewn cisterns which you did not dig, vineyards and olive trees which you did not plant, and you shall eat and be satisfied.
>
> "Then watch yourself, lest you forget the Lord who brought you from the land of Egypt, out of the house of slavery.
>
> "You shall fear only the Lord your God; and you shall worship Him, and swear by His name.
>
> "You shall not follow other gods, any of the gods of the peoples who surround you" (Deut. 6:10–14).

Before we examine this interesting section of Scripture and this relevant series of warnings, let's consider the third danger that emerges from these words.

3. *Assuming that size means strength.*

Here was a massive body of people, somewhere between one and two *million* individuals. Yet Moses announces to them, "Watch yourself!" Picture the scene. They have finally arrived at the promised land. Their future home was waiting for them—fertile fields, sufficient water, fruit trees and vineyards, homes ready to occupy (once the Canaanites were driven out), even entire cities all set for their arrival. All those things would be virtually laid in their laps.

Verse 10: ". . . cities . . . you did not build."

Verse 11: ". . . houses full of good things . . . you did not fill, . . . cisterns . . . you did not dig, vineyards . . . trees . . . you did not plant."

Verse 12: "Then watch yourself, lest you forget the Lord!"

Although they were a huge number of people and they would occupy ready-made cities and suburbs with all the comforts of home, none of the above guaranteed their strength. Even when Joshua was given a preinvasion briefing by the Lord (the account is found in Joshua 1:1–9) on no less than *three* occasions the commander-in-chief was told to "be strong and courageous" (vv. 6,7,9). In other words, their strength was not in their number or possessions, only the Lord could make them strong. If they got smug and proud, weakness would eat into their nation like acid. If they adopted the Canaanite culture and lost their distinctiveness in the morass of Gentile intermarriage, idolatry, and other forms of spiritual infidelity, they were goners! In a society overly impressed by size, this is a timely word for all of us. We would be foolish to believe that a family is strong because it has lots of children, that a city is strong simply because it's big, or a company is strong because its buildings are so extensive or because its employees are so numerous. That's the point—size and strength are not synonymous.

What's true of a family or a city or a company is equally true of a church. I'm not saying a large church *cannot* be strong, but only that it isn't automatically strong *because* it is large. Strength comes by being close, in touch, unmasked, and available to one another much more than by being big. Here are two examples of what I mean from Alan Loy McGinnis's book, *The Friendship Factor:*

> He was the world's ultimate mystery—so secretive, so reclusive, so enigmatic, that for more than 15 years no one could say for certain that he was alive, much less how he looked or behaved.
>
> Howard Hughes was one of the richest men in the world, with the destinies of thousands of people—perhaps even of governments—at his disposal, yet he lived a sunless, joyless, half-lunatic life. In his later years he fled from one resort hotel to another—Las Vegas, Nicaragua, Acapulco—and his physical appearance became odder and odder. His straggly beard hung down to his waist and his hair reached to the middle of his back. His fingernails were two inches long, and his toenails hadn't been trimmed for so long they resembled corkscrews.
>
> Hughes was married for 13 years to Jean Peters, one of the most beautiful women in the world. But never in that time were the two seen in public together, and there is no record of their ever having been photographed together. For a while they occupied separate bungalows at the Beverly Hills Hotel (at $175 per day each), and later she lived in an opulent and carefully guarded French Regency house atop a hill in Bel Air, making secretive and increasingly infrequent trips to be with Hughes in Las Vegas. They were divorced in 1970.
>
> "As far as I know," a Hughes confidant once said, "he's never loved any woman. It's sex, or a good secretary, or good box office—that is all a woman means to him." Hughes often said, "Every man has his price or a guy like me couldn't exist," yet no amount of money bought the affection of his associates. Most of his employees who have broken the silence report their disgust for him.
>
> Why was Hughes so isolated and so lonely? Why with almost unlimited money, hundreds of aides, and countless beautiful women available to him, was he so unloved?
>
> Simply because he chose to be.
>
> It is an old axiom that God gave us things to use and people to enjoy. Hughes never learned to enjoy people. He was too busy manipulating them. His interests were machines, gadgets, technology, airplanes, and money—interests so consuming as to exclude relationships.[3]

In the spring of 1887, a 20-year-old arrived in Tuscumbia, Alabama, to attempt the tutoring of a deaf-blind creature. The tutor's name was Anne Sullivan and the student's name was Helen Keller. They were to develop one of the most admired friendships of the century.

At seven, Helen Keller was a wild vixen who uttered unintelligible animal sounds. When in a rage, she would snatch dishes from the table and throw them and herself on the floor. More than one person had told Mrs. Keller that her child was an idiot.

For weeks Anne spelled words into Helen's small hand, but she could not break through to her consciousness. Then, on April 5, something wonderful happened. Here are Helen Keller's recollections of that day, written more than 60 years later:

> It happened at the well-house, where I was holding a mug under the spout. Annie pumped water into it, and when the water gushed out into my hand she kept spelling w-a-t-e-r into my other hand with her fingers. Suddenly I understood. Caught up in the first joy I had known since my illness, I reached out eagerly to Annie's ever-ready hand, begging for new words to identify whatever objects I touched. Spark after spark of meaning flew from hand to hand and, miraculously, affection was born. From the well-house there walked two enraptured beings calling each other "Helen" and "Teacher."

Anne Sullivan recognized that Helen was a prodigy and had unlimited possibilities for thinking and feeling. There was no question as to which of the two had the higher IQ. By the time she was 10, Helen was writing to famous persons in Europe in French. She quickly mastered five languages and displayed gifts which her teacher never pretended to have.

But did that change Anne Sullivan's devotion? Not so far as we know. She was satisfied to be Helen's companion and encourager, allowing her to be applauded by kings and presidents and to be her own unique personage. In short, she gave her friend room to grow.[4]

That brings us to the fourth danger for which we need to be alert.

4. *Living in the glow of yesterday instead of the challenge of tomorrow.* Listen again to God's counsel to Joshua: " 'Have I not commanded you? Be strong and courageous! Do not tremble

or be dismayed, for the Lord your God is with you wherever you go' " (Josh. 1:9).

There it is again—strength and courage come from the Lord. Then the commander turned and said to the Hebrews:

> "Pass through the midst of the camp and command the people, saying, 'Prepare provisions for yourselves, for within three days you are to cross this Jordan, to go in to possess the land which the Lord your God is giving you, to possess it' " (Josh. 1:11).

The command was for them to go on, to pursue new horizons. To face the future with renewed determination, not to live in the warm soft glow of the past. Those Hebrews were not instructed to relax and drift as they recalled the Exodus or their crossing the Red Sea, nor were they to spend their time erecting monuments and building shrines depicting their illustrious history. No, they were to tighten their belts and take on the challenge of conquering Canaan.

Ever been around a group of Christians who had adopted a holding pattern philosophy? You know, the old occupy-and-protect game plan rather than the pursue-new-territory-and-risk strategy. The sports world calls this "sitting on the lead" and coaches I know say that's lethal. It certainly is in a church. I cannot think of one Christian organization, either here in the United States or abroad, that decided to maintain the status quo yet remained fresh, creative, or vital very long after that decision was implemented. Neither do we as individuals. We advance or we retreat, but we don't remain static . . . not if we hope to stay in touch with our times and not if we are committed to open relationships and close friendships.

LONELINESS—EVEN AT "THE HOMESTEAD"

In this chapter we have considered several essential ingredients that make meaningful relationships take root, grow, and blossom. We have also exposed some of the dangers that lurk in the shadows—dangers that can sound the death knell to coming closer and thereby growing stronger together.

To illustrate just how effective our enemy is at keeping us isolated and distant, please return with me to The Homestead, that beautiful old resort in Virginia. Over fifty responsible, influential, and well-educated individuals are present . . . Christian statesmen embroiled in life-shaping decisions, at the hub of our nation's capital—good folks, solid citizens, family people you can't help but respect. They are folks who believe in our country and are willing to go on record for such basics as decency, integrity, patriotism, and godliness in our land. Most have been in the military or high-ranking political arenas for years. I didn't meet a novice in the whole gathering.

Do you know the single most-often mentioned dilemma they confessed to me? It wasn't public criticism or personality conflicts and pressure among their peers, or some issue they had believed in, fought for, and lost by a narrow margin. It wasn't even the news media, as vicious and insulting as that can be at times.

It was their own personal isolationism. Some came right out and called it loneliness. They may appear to be terribly involved. In fact, they are. Fourteen-to-sixteen-hour days are not that uncommon. There are staff and committee meetings and public speeches and congressional hearings and news conferences by the dozens. No doubt about it, they're busy. Public servants have little time to call their own. But meaningful friendships? Open and deep relationships? Other couples with whom they spend time, letting down their hair, sharing together, and entering into each others' lives? No. Without an exception, those who talked with me alone admitted this was woefully absent from their experience.

Time and again I heard words like "superficial," "shallow," "skin deep," and "formal" as they candidly described their horizontal relationships. Wives of these public figures admitted, during our three-day retreat, that they live ultraprivate, guarded lives . . . and in some cases, it has really taken a toll on their children. It's hard for families to flourish in secret caves.

At supper one evening with a popular Cabinet member and

his wife, I decided to come up front and ask them a direct question regarding this subject. I leaned toward the statesman and said, "Honestly, how deep are your friendships? Do you have even *one* person or couple with whom you can be yourselves—totally open and unguarded?"

The answer came quickly. After admitting, "No—no close friends, Chuck," he held out his hand, pointed his index finger in my direction, then pulled up his thumb with about an eighth of an inch of daylight showing in between and added, "All our relationships are about *that* deep." I looked at his wife and gave her one of my is-that-the-truth? looks. Without hesitation she nodded, "That's no exaggeration. We're close to no one." I told them that I believed they were not that unusual, certainly not in Washington, D.C. Then I mentioned I was in the process of writing this book. They smiled with approval, as if to say, "Good! Folks like us need all the help we can get." Who would've ever guessed?

As I think back, I find it ironic that all those capable Christian people, servants to the public, admitted their loneliness and isolation at a place named "The Homestead."

DISCUSSION IDEAS AND QUESTIONS

- Spend a few minutes discussing the three "essential ingredients" of developing close relationships with other people:
  - —Admission of need for others
  - —Cultivation of deeper relationships
  - —Firm commitment to assimilation.
- Of the three, which one is the most difficult for *you* personally. Explain why.
- Read 1 Corinthians 12:14–21 aloud. Talk about the importance of these verses.
- One of the dangers connected with getting closer to others relates to the high-profile role of the leader . . . almost to the point of exalting the leader more than the Lord. What can leaders do to encourage assimilation rather than thwart it?
- In working our way through Deuteronomy 6, we discovered that it is easy to lose sight of the ultimate objective. Pause and consider the objective(s) of your small group. Write down two or three (not more than four) that everyone can agree on. Periodically review them to help you stay on target.
- We may be quick to ask "Wonder why public servants live such isolated lives?" when, in reality, we do the same thing. What are you doing to keep that from occurring in your life? If someone looked into your eyes and asked, "Do you have a close meaningful relationship with one or more people?" what would you say?
- Pray for those who serve our country in places of high-level responsibility. Ask God to help them cultivate nonsuperficial friendships. If you know the names of a few such leaders, call their names in prayer.

4

Operation
Assimilation

CLOSE RELATIONSHIPS aren't automatic. They are the direct result of time, energy, and cultivation.

The first time it really came clear to me that we naturally relate to one another on a superficial level, I was standing in line in cap and gown, about to graduate from seminary. Here we stood as a class of young men, having completed four tough years of graduate school education and training. Although weary and anxious to get on with our lives, most of us were seized with a touch of nostalgia. We'd never be together again. Within a matter of hours we would be separated by miles, and in some cases, by continents and oceans.

Perhaps that is what prompted the man standing behind me to reach around me and tap the fella standing in front of me on the shoulder. He asked, rather embarrassingly, "Now what was your full name?"

You need to understand that our graduating class was not

that large, less than seventy in all. We had been through four consecutive years of classes (some of them quite small), chapel services every day (we sat alphabetically), out-of-school sports activities, picnics, dinners, and ministry involvements. And most of our contact was on a campus no more than one square block in size . . . many of us living right on campus for at least part, if not all, of that time. Yet one man didn't even know the first and last name of another man who sat only two seats away from him for four long years. Seems incredible, I realize, but it did actually happen.

Popular psychologist and one of my dear personal friends, Dr. James Dobson, tells a similar story, only far more tragic than mine. He was a visiting lecturer at a seminary where he had spoken on the subject of self-esteem. His emphasis was that we cannot assume people have a healthy view of themselves just because they are studying for vocational Christian service. In fact, some struggle with this problem far more intensely than we can possibly imagine.

> I was recently invited to conduct a lecture series for faculty and students at a seminary. It seemed appropriate that I talk to these future ministers about the subject of inferiority, since they would soon be dealing with many such problems in their own congregations. During the course of my first address, I relayed a story of "Danny." Danny was a distressed high-school student whose grief over his inadequacy became intolerable and eventually turned to anger. After I had spoken that day, I received the following anonymous letter:

> Dear Dr. Dobson—
> I am one of the "Dannys" you spoke of in chapel today. Believe me, for I have experienced this for as long as I can remember. It is a miserable way to live.
> Yes, I'm a student at the seminary, but that doesn't make the problem any less acute. Through the years, particularly the last five, I have periodically gained a revived hope that somehow(?) this problem can be overcome—go away or something. Then to my great disappointment, I find it is still very much a part of me. That's when I lose hope of ever conquering it.

I want to be a minister of the gospel and feel that this is
God's will. *At the same time I am aware of the paralyzing effect
this deep problem has upon me.* I want so badly to be adequate
so that I could better serve God and others.

I wish I could talk with you, even for a short time. However,
I realize your busy schedule. At any rate, thank you for coming
to the seminary.

> Sincerely,
> A troubled seminarian

Since this broken young man had not identified himself publicly,
I read and discussed his letter with the student body the following
morning. Many of the three hundred young men who were present
seemed moved by his words; for some, it undoubtedly reflected
their own predicament as well. Following my lecture that morning,
the "troubled seminarian" came and introduced himself to me.
He stood with tears streaming down his cheeks as he spoke of
the great sense of inadequacy he had experienced since early child-
hood. Later, an administrator of the seminary told me that this
young man was the last member of the student body whom he
would have expected to feel this way. As I have observed so many
times, this sense of inferiority is the best-kept secret of the year.
It is harbored deep inside, where it can gnaw on the soul.

Sitting in the audience that same day was another student with
the same kind of problems. However, he did not write me a letter.
He never identified himself in any way. But three weeks after I
left, he hanged himself in the basement of his apartment. One
of the four men with whom he lived called long distance to inform
me of the tragedy. He stated, deeply shaken, that the dead student's roommates were so unaware of his problems that he hung
there five days before he was missed![1]

The first time I read those words my mouth dropped open and
I almost gasped out loud. The suicide was, of course, tragic
beyond description, but to think that the student's *roommates*
didn't miss him for five days seems absolutely unbelievable. If
that can happen in a school where dedicated Christians are sup-
posedly in close contact with one another, it can certainly happen
in your neighborhood . . . on your job . . . in your church
. . . yes, and even in your home. That's a major reason I was

prompted to write this book. Somehow, in our hurry-up, high-tech times, people can drop through the cracks and nobody even notices.

ASSIMILATION DEFINED

Close, open relationships are therefore vital. A glib "Hi, how are ya" must be replaced with genuine concern. The key term is *assimilation*. You won't get much help from Webster if you're searching for a definition. I know, I checked. Are you ready?

> . . . the incorporation or conversion of nutrients into proto-plasm that in animals follows digestion and absorption and in higher plants involves both photosynthesis and root absorption.[2]

Uh, nope . . . that's not exactly what I have in mind. We're talking about people in society, not animals in the field or plants in a garden. When I use the word in this book, I'm referring to people reaching out to one another.

Being absorbed in the function of the family of God
   as a participant (rather than a spectator)
      . . . relating to
         . . . working with
            . . . caring for others
            whom I know and love.

That would be my definition of assimilation. As I read it over, I see written between the lines the reminder:

This
  is
    not
      automatic.
        I am personally responsible.
          So are you!

Somehow we have picked up the erroneous idea that open relationships and consistent assimilation will just start happening. If you like to fantasize, you could entertain the thought that some technically gifted inventor will one day devise an electronic gizmo that will solve our tendency toward isolation. It won't happen. Don't wait for a new video game or home computer or hand-held calculator that will tear down our relational barriers. On the contrary, those things seem to accomplish quite the opposite. If you question that, stroll through the local video arcade. Nobody relates to anybody!

In his mind-stretching work, *Megatrends*, John Naisbitt addresses and assaults what he calls "the danger of the technofix mentality."

> When we fall into the trap of believing or, more accurately, hoping that technology will solve all our problems, we are actually abdicating the high touch of personal responsibility. Our technological fantasies illustrate the point. We are always awaiting the new magical pill that will enable us to eat all the fattening food we want, and not gain weight; burn all the gasoline we want, and not pollute the air; live as immoderately as we choose, and not contract either cancer or heart disease.
>
> In our minds, at least, technology is always on the verge of liberating us from personal discipline and responsibility. Only it never does and it never will.
>
> The more high technology around us, the more the need for human touch.[3]

When our congregation got serious about close relationships and assimilation, we decided that they weren't going to happen *to* us, but *among* us. Otherwise, we would erode into an uninvolved body of spectators who come and watch a few folks "up front" do their thing. Being the senior pastor, I felt the need to address these things from the pulpit, which I did in a series of Sunday morning sermons I entitled "Congregational Relationships." Not a very creative title, but the content and the consistency of the series (twelve messages in all) began to have an effect. People realized there was much more to Christianity than sitting, singing, listening, and leaving. Our youth and adult ministries got even more involved in implementing ways to "assimilate" those who desired closer relationships. During-the-week, small-group gatherings proliferated like never before, and a contagious spirit of enthusiasm was reborn.

The old "saved, sanctified, galvanized" mentality was no longer satisfying. Mere pew sitting and sermon sampling by uninvolved isolationists were now being challenged as we allowed God's Word to inform and reprove us. Without in any way suggesting that I spoke out against a strong pulpit, my emphasis was that there should be other things just as strong—strong relationships, strong music and worship. My emphasis was on caring for others, involving ourselves in needs around us, and opening our lives to one another in smaller groups. In other words, we needed to be setting a pace in more areas than the preaching ministry. We were (and still are) committed to biblical exposition—perhaps more than ever in our history—but now we are hoping to follow through in some areas of biblical application. I'm pleased to say that it's working beautifully.

How the Ancient Hebrews Did It

So much for us . . . let's step back into the time tunnel once again and see if all this has biblical roots. Maybe a quick review will help.

- The Hebrews had left the familiar surroundings of Egypt, and God had shown Himself faithful as He led them, protected them, and fed them (even though they grumbled).
- The Jewish nomads remained disjointed and lacking in unity as they worked their way from Egypt to Canaan.
- After spying out the land, they were *again* divided. Some said, "Let's go, we can conquer!" But many more said, "No, let's return."
- For almost forty years they wandered around in the wilderness until the entire older generation died off. With the new generation came a new leader—Joshua.

That's where we take up the story.

> Now it came about after the death of Moses the servant of the Lord that the Lord spoke to Joshua the son of Nun, Moses' servant, saying, "Moses My servant is dead; now therefore arise, cross this Jordan, you and all this people, to the land which I am giving to them, to the sons of Israel.
>
> "Every place on which the sole of your foot treads, I have given it to you, just as I spoke to Moses.
>
> "From the wilderness and this Lebanon, even as far as the great river, the river Euphrates, all the land of the Hittites, and as far as the Great Sea toward the setting of the sun, will be your territory.
>
> "No man will be able to stand before you all the days of your life. Just as I have been with Moses, I will be with you; I will not fail you or forsake you" (Josh. 1:1–5).

That's what I would call reassurance. Such inspiring words would naturally prompt motivation. But they needed more than motivation. They needed to be melted together into a solidly committed unit, ready to invade and conquer Canaan. As I read through this chapter, no less than four principles leap off the page, each one illustrating how "assimilated" they were once they marched securely into Canaan.

1. *They relied on God for their future.* God and Joshua were in close communication (v. 1). The plan was clearly set forth (vv. 2–4), and the people were promised success (v. 5). It was God's voice against the odds. Unintimidated, Joshua and the people believed. Although outnumbered, they pressed on.

This kind of faithfulness reminds me of the Reformation when a relatively small band of men deliberately placed their faith in an infinitely awesome God. What followed didn't simply "happen" . . . it was the direct result of men like Luther, Calvin, Zwingli, Savonarola, Melanchthon, Knox, and a dozen or so more who relied on God for their future. The same could be said of the Great Awakening in England or the Second Awakening in America. Those who became a part of those movements were committed to the living God and to His unfailing promises.

But that's history, some of it centuries old. How about some more relevant examples. Do we have such? Indeed. To list only a few:

- "Uncle Cam" Townsend and the Wycliffe Bible Translators
- Dawson Trotman and The Navigators
- M. R. DeHaan and the Radio Bible Class and Day of Discovery
- Henrietta Mears and Forest Home Christian Conference Center
- Bill Bright and Campus Crusade for Christ, International
- Billy Graham and his Worldwide Evangelistic Crusades and Films.

I'll not take the time to mention others equally deserving of our attention and respect. Those names stand out like modern-day Joshuas, people who relied on God and created a following of unified, committed disciples of the Savior. The good news is this: History *continues* to be written. Who knows? Someday your name might appear in such a list as you, too, become a pacesetter.

There is more. Let's look at a second principle which illustrates how assimilated the Hebrews were as they marched into Canaan.

2. *They accepted the challenge without fear of failure.* No less than four times we read that they were to be strong, courageous, confident, fearless (vv. 6,7,9,18). In fact, the ninth verse comes right out and says, "Do not tremble or be dismayed." Today we would say, "Don't get shook up. Don't let intimidation do a number on you."

Anytime (yes, *any* time) there is a new furrow to be plowed, a new path to be cleared, a new idea to be tried, or a new strategy to be implemented, fear of failure stands tall as a giant. And all too often, it pushes its way in and gains a foothold. It has been my observation that the greater the possibility of impact, the greater the fear of failure ahead of time. That is what makes the Canaan invasion so exciting. It was so incredible, so humanly impossible, it had all the makings of a classic, *Guinness Book of World Records* failure.

How often we Christians unknowingly tip our hands. We pray with beseeching hands lifted high, "Oh, Lord, almighty and omnipotent God, who knows no barrier and who cannot fail, we present this need to you today in prayer. . . ." And then immediately on the heels of that theologically powerful petition, we frown as we look around the table and say, "Gentlemen, the situation we face today is completely hopeless . . . *nothing* can be done." When will we ever learn that there are no hopeless situations, only people who have grown hopeless about them? What appears as an unsolvable problem to us is actually a rather exhilarating challenge. People who inspire others are those who see invisible bridges at the end of dead-end streets.

There was a Cabinet meeting in London during the darkest days of the Second World War. France had just capitulated. Prime Minister Churchill outlined the situation in its starkest colors. Quite literally, the tiny British Isles stood alone. Grim faces stared back at him in stoic silence. Despair and thoughts of surrender were written in their looks. The visionary statesman momentarily remained silent, lit a cigar, showed a hint of a smile, and with a twinkle in his eye, responded to that dispirited company of officials, "Gentlemen, I find it rather inspiring." He was the one who, on another occasion, said, "Nothing in life is so exhilirating as to be shot at without result." What a great line! No wonder people followed the man. Fear of failure never entered his mind.

When we read on in the Joshua account, we discover that the Hebrews took courage and got their stuff together:

> Then Joshua commanded the officers of the people, saying, "Pass through the midst of the camp and command the people, saying, 'Prepare provisions for yourselves, for within three days you are to cross this Jordan, to go in to possess the land which the Lord your God is giving you, to possess it.' "
> And to the Reubenites and to the Gadites and to the half-tribe of Manasseh, Joshua said, "Remember the word which Moses

the servant of the Lord commanded you, saying, 'The Lord your God gives you rest, and will give you this land.'

"Your wives, your little ones, and your cattle shall remain in the land which Moses gave you beyond the Jordan but you shall cross before your brothers in battle array, all your valiant warriors, and shall help them, until the Lord gives your brothers rest, as He gives you, and they also possess the land which the Lord your God is giving them. Then you shall return to your own land, and possess that which Moses the servant of the Lord gave you beyond the Jordan toward the sunrise" (Josh. 1:10–15).

As I read these words, I observe a couple or three things they did: They prepared provisions for themselves, they ignored tribal distinctions (no discrimination), and they demonstrated no selfishness—they helped one another. Isn't that exciting? An entire fighting force—a mighty army—moving ahead without fear of failure. By faith, they moved out.

> Everyone who starts a new venture—whether a Charles Lindbergh carefully planning to cross the Atlantic, a Henry Ford launching an infant industry into the mainstream of world transportation, or a homemaker deciding to go back to school or start a business—faces certain fears, inner struggles, and temptations to quit. But there are ways of planning and of handling adversity and setbacks which have often made the difference between those who have risked and succeeded and those who have never really begun.[4]

Those are the words of a man who literally turned garbage into a multimillion dollar business mainly because he refused to be intimidated by the fear of failure.

As I think about those ancient Jews and the magnificent way God assimilated and mobilized them into a secure fighting force, I realize a third principle was put into operation.

3. *They ignored their differences and closed ranks in unity.* It is nothing short of remarkable how powerful and how effective a body of people can become when concern for who gets the credit or the emphasis on rank and status or talk about differences

is dropped. These Hebrews, once they heard Joshua's game plan and realized it was actually *God's* strategy for victory, rallied around the plan and promised their allegiance.

> And they answered Joshua, saying, "All that you have commanded us we will do, and wherever you send us we will go.
> "Just as we obeyed Moses in all things, so we will obey you; only may the Lord your God be with you, as He was with Moses.
> "Anyone who rebels against your command and does not obey your words in all that you command him, shall be put to death; only be strong and courageous" (Josh. 1:16–18).

Don't forget, these are words of affirmation declared spontaneously from the lips of those whose history was checkered with failure, unbelief, and defeat. But all that was past. It was now time to close ranks as they forgot their differences. What a refreshing atmosphere is created when God's people march together in unity toward the same objective!

Perhaps you remember one of the verses from the nineteenth-century gospel song, "Onward, Christian Soldiers" by Sabine Baring-Gould:

> Like a mighty army
> Moves the church of God;
> Brothers, we are treading
> Where the saints have trod;
>
> We are not divided,
> All one body we,
> One in hope and doctrine,
> One in charity.

How can there be such a spirit today? Such unity? It's neither mysterious nor complicated. The adversary would have us believe there's no way. He will do *anything* to divide us. But you and I know that all that is required to maintain incessant, invincible confidence is a willingness to focus on the many things we have in common rather than the few things that make us different.

Assimilation and pettiness cannot coexist. I love (and often quote) the words of the sixteenth-century theologian Philipp Melanchthon, "In essentials, unity; in nonessentials, liberty; in all things, charity." I suggest you make that your motto of the year. "We are not divided, all one body we!"

> John Wesley and George Whitefield were good friends in their earlier years, Wesley having begun his outdoor preaching ministry at Whitefield's encouragement. As time went on the men disagreed, with Whitefield leaning more heavily toward Calvinism than his younger friend's Arminianism. When Whitefield died, Wesley was asked if he expected to see Dr. Whitefield in heaven. In exaggerated but honest respect he answered, "No, he'll be so near the throne of God that men like me will never even get a glimpse of him!" Though differing, they did not lose their sense of oneness in Christ.[5]

It has been my observation that well-meaning but narrow-minded evang :cals in this generation have spent far too much time camping on a few differences—and thereby opening our ranks to disunity and petty infighting—and not enough time accentuating the vast number of things that link us together. And the result has been weakness rather than strength—a divided, splintered, fractured body of Christian cripples instead of that "mighty army" of crack troops.

In the fall of 1981, I was speaking at a banquet in a city where almost two thousand Christian people had gathered. The spirit was electric with excitement as folks realized we were not alone in the battle. We had enjoyed a delicious meal and some superb music. God was using His truth to cement our hearts together in a rare blend of unity and love. Assimilation was happening as relational masks and professional status were being replaced with a renewed commitment to one another. It was wonderful!

Suddenly, the meeting was disrupted by a young man who pushed his way into the room. He began to shout his disapproval and proclaim some particular conviction which he held. He was asked to leave as people stared in disbelief. He refused, continuing his diatribe at top volume. His face was stern and his voice shrill. Finally, after he was forcibly removed from the meeting, we were able to continue and complete the evening, though the spirit of unity and mutual enthusiasm was never fully recovered. I found out later that the same man—a fellow believer— regularly does such things. He believes it is his calling. He is convinced he has "the gift of rebuking" (try to find *that* in Scripture!), so he travels around disrupting meetings and declaring how wrong other Christians are who do not agree with his particular (and in my opinion *insignificant*) doctrinal slant.

By the way, as we left the banquet the man's stern-faced disciples were outside with leaflets and propaganda brochures verbally taking issue with the things that had been done and said at our banquet. As my wife and I drove away, we felt sick at heart. It was a never-to-be-forgotten proof that sincere people can become tools in the hands of the adversary, all the while thinking they are doing the work of God. On more than a few occasions since then I have heard of the same man doing the same thing in similar settings. Until we are big enough to ignore our few differences and close ranks, the strength brought on by unity will not be there. And the enemy will continue dancing for joy. That brings us to the fourth principle illustrated by the Hebrews as they crossed into the promised land.

4. *They abandoned themselves to the plan as they fixed their attention on the Lord.* Take a close, final look at these words once again. See if you don't detect true motivation:

> And they answered Joshua, saying, "All that you have commanded us we will do, and wherever you send us we will go.
> "Just as we obeyed Moses in all things, so we will obey you; only may the Lord your God be with you, as He was with Moses" (Josh. 1:16–17).

That's abandonment! "All . . . wherever. . . ." And talk about willing obedience! ". . . we will do . . . we will go . . . we will obey. . . ." And how do you think Joshua felt when they promised him the same loyalty they had given to Moses? How could they have been so willing? What prompted such wholesale commitment? Aren't these the offspring of that mob of independent, stubborn, and spoiled nomads who struck out against Moses and resisted the Lord in the wilderness? Indeed they are! Then, how can we explain the change? What could possibly be powerful enough to turn the hearts of these people? Their eyes were fully on the Lord. He was now in focus. They saw Him at work. As a result, their entire perspective had changed. He was giving the drumbeat, and they were marching in step with the cadence. There was no reluctance; they now wanted Him and His will. With that mindset, phenomenal adjustments and adaptations are possible. But let us all be warned, without it, forget about being drawn closer. Operation assimilation becomes a distant dream, abandonment becomes a joke, and unity, an impossibility. Trite though it may sound, it's true—not until our eyes are on the Lord will we be big enough to overlook differences and open enough to adapt and adjust.

IMPLICATIONS AND RAMIFICATIONS

Let me close this chapter by mentioning three practical areas of our lives that are affected when we get serious about assimilation: our churches, our acquaintances, our one-on-one relationships.

In Our Churches

For us to go on, for us to get the job done, we need to pull together, ignoring our petty differences. Let's not let the enemy do a number on us. If he is successful in dividing our interests and fracturing our fellowship, the world has more evidence that Christianity does not work. And don't think the world isn't ready to pounce on our disunity.

Just this morning on the front page of the *Los Angeles Times* (circulation well over one million), there's a picture and a lead article of a church doing battle with the state over its tax status. And, believe it or not, on the front page of Part II, in the Orange County Edition, the same newspaper has placed in headline print, "300 MEMBERS SPLINTER FROM CHURCH," and three more columns are used to cover the story of a church split that has occurred in a large, highly visible ministry that is now fighting within its own ranks.[6] Tragically, hundreds of thousands of non-Christians will become more convinced than ever that Christianity lacks the very things they are in need of— love, affirmation, and integrity.

Among Our Acquaintances

For us to be involved, we must be willing to reach out and risk relating. This won't "just happen." If my friend in graduate school wasn't aware of a man's name after four years of similar activity in a close geographical context, I seriously doubt that others in a much broader base would be that much different. May I urge you? Risk reaching. Take the initiative. Walk a few feet to your neighbor's yard. Or start with a simple and a warm, sincere wave of the hand. Find some common ground of mutual interest and use that as a basis of conversation. Open up. Be warm and transparent. You may be pleasantly surprised by the results.

One on One

If assimilation is ever to make the journey from theory to reality, we'll have to be willing to adapt and adjust the closer we get. One-on-one sooner or later requires give-and-take. Don't kid yourself, this is where the rubber and the road meet. And sometimes the road is uphill. Reuben Welch so aptly describes the journey in his poem, "We Really Do Need Each Other."

> You know something—
> we're all just people who need each other.

We're all learning
and we've all got a long journey ahead of us.
We've got to go together
and if it takes us until Jesus comes
we better stay together
we better help each other.
And I dare say
that by the time we get there
all the sandwiches will be gone
and all the chocolate will be gone
and all the water will be gone
and all the backpacks will be empty.
But no matter how long it takes us
we've got to go together.
Because that's how it is
in the body of Christ.
It's all of us
in love
in care
in support
in mutuality—
we really do need each other.[7]

Remember what is written between the lines:

This
is
not
automatic.
I am personally responsible.
So are you.

DISCUSSION IDEAS AND QUESTIONS

- Time and again we were reminded in chapter 4 that close relationships are not automatic. Nor are they necessarily easy to develop. Spend a few minutes discussing some of your own experiences that prove this is true.
- High-tech times seem to result in superficial conversations and unsatisfying relationships. Why? Do you see any tie-in between shallow neighbor relations and families who frequently move? Can you cite some examples?
- Let's think now about your church and the matter of assimilation. In light of what you read in this chapter, how could you help draw people closer together? Be specific. Think of realistic ways to break down barriers and convey Christ's love and affirmation.
- The first chapter of Joshua throbs with fresh excitement. We found four principles from the lines of these eighteen verses. Go back and review them. Which one speaks most directly to you? Explain why.
- Toward the end of the chapter we focused in on the subject of unity. Remember the John Wesley–George Whitefield story? Discuss its implications. What impresses you the most about the humility of Wesley?
- How's your A.Q. (Adaptability Quotient)? Share an occasion when you adjusted your life to help someone else—or they did that for you—and the benefits that resulted. Pray for someone who needs to be encouraged and helped. Make yourself available.

5

United and
Invincible

THERE ONCE LIVED a king who loved to write music. And, even though he has been dead for centuries, his songs live on. This king's name was David. And today we call his songs psalms. Although ancient, some of his pieces have a relevance about them that make them timeless. Listen to this one. It's one of his best:

> How good and pleasant it is
>   when brothers live together in unity!
> It is like precious oil poured on the head,
>   running down on the beard . . .
>   down upon the collar of his robes (Ps. 133:1–2, NIV).

If there had been a *Hit Parade of Psalms* back then, that's one I would have voted for. The longer I live, the more I realize the value of that imperative, "brothers live together in unity."

As David wrote, unity is like oil. It removes the friction in relationships so that brothers and sisters can live closely without fighting. Difficult as it may be for some to believe it, God planned it so that we might relate together even though we are different in taste, preference, style, culture, color, education, and language. It is "good and pleasant" that we live in unity—all our differences notwithstanding.

Some jokesters tell about a group of theologians who were discussing predestination and free will. The longer they talked, the hotter it got. And, as you might expect, the dissidents split into two groups. One poor fella didn't know which he believed, so he slipped into the ranks of the predestination crowd. They challenged him as to why he was there. "I came of my own free will," he answered innocently. Frowning, they responded, *"Free will?* You can't join us. You get over there!" He retreated to the opposite group and faced the same challenging spirit. "Listen, I was *sent* here," he answered honestly. "Leave!" they demanded. "You can't join us unless you come of your own free will!"

Poor guy, he needed some of that oil David wrote about. And so do a lot of other dear souls who have spun into their own isolated orbit, having been kicked around by various narrow-minded, exclusive groups.

BIBLICAL BASIS OF UNITY

According to the Scriptures, all Christians are knit together in an invisible bond. The bond transcends personality and geography . . . or perhaps it's safer to say, it *should.* A believer in mid-America is linked with another believer in the heart of Brazil or Norway and just as closely knitted with a Christian in a dormitory in Oxford University or, for that matter, with a suffering, persecuted Russian believer in a slave camp behind the Iron Curtain.

The Apostles' Creed calls this bond "the communion of the saints." The great apostle Paul refers to it in the first Corinthian letter as the "body," as he declares that we are "members of it" (1 Cor. 12:27). To remind ourselves of this united bond that links believers together, our congregation in Fullerton often blends voice and heart as we sing the lovely chorus of worship:

> We are one in the bond of love;
> We are one in the bond of love;
> We have joined our spirits with the Spirit of God;
> We are one in the bond of love.[1]

What makes that bond possible? How is it that you and I are united in the same body as "members" one with another? That answer is extremely important—it is Jesus Christ. He, alone, brings the body together. As the Head, He is in charge of all the body members. He, therefore, makes the blend of unity possible. "He is also head of the body, the church; and He is the beginning, the first-born from the dead; so that He Himself might come to have first place in everything" (Col. 1:18).

Think in terms of the familiar mathematical axiom, "Things equal to the same thing are equal to each other." An everyday illustration would be a roomful of pianos, all of which are out of tune. What a maddening job it would be if the piano tuner tried to tune each instrument according to the others in the room or, worse, according to his own "inner pitch." He would be tightening this string and loosening that one in such a hit-or-miss manner that he would *never* get the job done. Instead, he begins with a tuning fork. That simple one-tone instrument becomes the standard for each piano in the room. And pianos tuned to the same thing are tuned to each other.

Wouldn't it be wonderful if it were that simple! But in the body, we're not talking about multistringed pianos but rather multifaceted people with different bents, temperaments, levels of maturity, and backgrounds. Jesus, knowing this was true, once prayed concerning our need for unity. That prayer is recorded in the seventeenth chapter of John. In fact, the entire chapter is His prayer. An outline of John 17 would look like this:

- In verses one through five, He prays for Himself.
- In verses six through nineteen, He prays for His disciples.
- In verses twenty through twenty-six, He prays for all those yet to believe on Him—including us.

And what is the theme of that prayer? Obviously, *unity*. Let's look closer:

Verse 21: "That they may all be one."

Verse 22: "That they may be one, just as We are one."

Verse 23: "That they may be perfected in unity."

Literally, the last reference could be rendered "that they may be perfected *into a unit.*" How beautifully the New International Version translates verse 23: ". . . May they be brought to complete unity to let the world know that you sent me and have loved them even as you have loved me."

What has happened to our unity? This simple plan, so beautifully articulated by Jesus and so wonderfully begun in the first century, has been woefully complicated and confused by man. Denominations now number into the *hundreds*. Even the restrictive ranks of evangelicalism are divided into more than thirty various groups, all confessing a common faith in the Lord Jesus Christ. Surely the world scratches its head at that. And lest you think denominational lines or religious labels are not drawn that tightly, stop and ask people on the street if they are Christians. Chances are good they will identify themselves not as a Christian or non-Christian, but as a Methodist or Presbyterian or Catholic or Baptist or Charismatic or some such identification.

Have you stopped to think lately what God's opinion of all these categories must be? We have drifted a long way from Jesus' prayer, "that they may be perfected into a unit." And at times when unity *is* present, it's a cold formalism, more of a rigid requirement than a free-flowing spontaneity. As one Christian admitted to me with a smile, "Unity? Yeah, my church has unity. We're *frozen* together!" Behind that smile his teeth were set firm. No, that's not the unity Christ wants in His body. The unity He desires is one that strengthens and encourages us in our pilgrimage. In fact, when that unity is present, we begin to walk in such confidence that there's a definite hint of invincibility in our faith. It's all part of the way God arranged it. We even see it illustrated in the lives of those Hebrews who invaded Canaan under Joshua's leadership.

THE HEBREWS: HORIZONTAL UNITY, VERTICAL VICTORY

As we travel through the pages of ancient history, we find ample evidence that God honors a spirit of unity among His people. Let's return to the book of Joshua and pick up the story of the Hebrews right where we left off at the end of the previous chapter.

> And they answered Joshua, saying, "All that you have commanded us we will do, and wherever you send us we will go.
> "Just as we obeyed Moses in all things, so we will obey you; only may the Lord your God be with you, as He was with Moses.
> "Anyone who rebels against your command and does not obey your words in all that you command him, shall be put to death; only be strong and courageous" (Josh. 1:16–18).

These three verses throb with anticipation. They are the words of a motivated body of people. Within their response are promises of cooperation ("we will do"), availability ("we will go"), commitment ("we will obey"), loyalty ("anyone who rebels . . . shall be put to death"), and encouragement ("be strong and courageous"). What an unusual twist! The people are encouraging the leader. That's one of the many by-products of a unified body of people—their eyes are off themselves and on others.

If you don't think that is rare, here are a few questions worth consideration:

- How many congregations have you ever been a part of (or *heard* of) who regularly encouraged their pastor?
- How often have you witnessed students in the classroom who encouraged and affirmed the teacher?

- When was the last time you saw on television or read in the newspaper where the news media spoke unanimously in appreciation of the President?
- Look at your place of occupation. Is it a common thing to hear employees speak favorably of their supervisors?
- I wonder how many who serve on the city council or school board in your community can remember the last time a group of citizens gathered for one reason . . . simply to tell them "thanks, nice job." (I'm sure you're smiling.)

We are all much better at complaining than affirming—much better at criticizing than encouraging. Those folks in Joshua's day were a refreshing exception to the rule. And to make matters even better, when it came time to put action to words, they proved the sincerity of their allegiance. Let me show you what I mean.

AN UNUSUAL STRATEGY ACCEPTED WITHOUT RESISTANCE

Let's take a close look at the sixth chapter of Joshua. Combat is around the corner. In comparison to the tough resilient forces of Canaan, those Hebrews must have appeared as a rag-tag bunch of unorganized nomads. But there was one giant factor that made the difference. They had Jehovah on their side. And He wasn't about to let his reputation be ruined by a pack of godless pagans.

> Now Jericho was tightly shut because of the sons of Israel; no one went out and no one came in.
> And the Lord said to Joshua, "See, I have given Jericho into your hand, with its king and the valiant warriors (vv. 1–2).

Jericho must have appeared formidable. A massive stone wall no less than three stories high and eighteen feet thick surrounded that city full of "valiant warriors." Yet Joshua was given a promise, "I have given Jericho into your hands." But how? Some secret weapon? Some powerful explosive? No. Just an unusual strategy.

> "And you shall march around the city, all the men of war circling the city once. You shall do so for six days.
> "Also seven priests shall carry seven trumpets of rams' horns before the ark; then on the seventh day you shall march around the city seven times, and the priests shall blow the trumpets.
> "And it shall be that when they make a long blast with the rams' horn, and when you hear the sound of the trumpet, all the people shall shout with a great shout; and the wall of the city will fall down flat, and the people will go up every man straight ahead" (Josh. 6:3–5).

Now *that's* a novel idea. No big deal. Just believe God and do exactly what He says. If He says the wall will fall, count on it. He's awfully good at walls, you know. Nobody laughed. Nobody even snickered. I mean, those folks were willing and ready! They'd wandered in the wilderness long enough to know better than to question God's plan.

> So Joshua the son of Nun called the priests and said to them, "Take up the ark of the covenant, and let seven priests carry seven trumpets of rams' horns before the ark of the Lord."
> Then he said to the people, "Go forward, and march around the city, and let the armed men go on before the ark of the Lord."
> And it was so, that when Joshua had spoken to the people, the seven priests carrying the seven trumpets of rams' horns before the Lord went forward and blew the trumpets; and the ark of the covenant of the Lord followed them.
> And the armed men went before the priests who blew the trumpets, and the rear guard came after the ark, while they continued to blow the trumpets.
> But Joshua commanded the people, saying, "You shall not shout nor let your voice be heard, nor let a word proceed out of your mouth, until the day I tell you, 'Shout!' Then you shall shout!"
> So he had the ark of the Lord taken around the city, circling

it once, then they came into the camp and spent the night in the camp (Josh. 6:6–11).

Then came that final trip.

> Then it came about on the seventh day that they rose early at the dawning of the day and marched around the city in the same manner seven times; only on that day they marched around the city seven times.
> And it came about at the seventh time, when the priests blew the trumpets, Joshua said to the people, "Shout! For the Lord has given you the city" (Josh. 6:15–16).

> So the people shouted, and priests blew the trumpets; and it came about, when the people heard the sound of the trumpet, that the people shouted with a great shout and the wall fell down flat, so that the people went up into the city, every man straight ahead, and they took the city.
> And they utterly destroyed everything in the city, both man and woman, young and old, and ox and sheep and donkey, with the edge of the sword (Josh. 6:20–21).

Talk about invincible! When they began to see and hear the walls of Jericho crumble, those Hebrews must have smiled with indescribable delight. Especially after they had obeyed the Lord's orders so perfectly. What a game plan! March, blow, scream—then stand back. I love the utter ridiculousness of it all . . . from a human point of view, that is. Whoever heard of such a weird strategy? In our day of high-tech sophistication, who would ever consider cooperating? But the good news is that, when we *do* obey, unusual though the plan may seem, only God can get the glory.

When our church congregation decided to relocate and build a new facility from scratch, one formidable piece of the puzzle required massive faith—selling the old facility. It was during a financial slump. Furthermore, who was in the market for the ultimate white elephant of real estate, a used church (and I do mean *used*)? God made it clear that all we should do is put it on the market and trust Him. There was no need for panic, no need to worry about the odds. Just pray and refuse all temptations to manipulate or manufacture a manmade plan. Or, in the words of Psalm 46:10 (a verse I must have repeated to myself fifty or more times during the long months of waiting): "Cease striving and know that I am God."

We came right down to the wire. In fact, it was the final week. Sunday was the ultimate deadline. No breakthrough. On Saturday, the day before, a small unassuming body of believers contacted one of our church officers. They came by and looked things over. They asked if it would be possible to visit again on Sunday afternoon. When they returned and said, "We want it," the walls of our financial Jericho fell down flat.

Those who stand united become an invincible force through whom God does His greatest work. The secret, remember, is closed ranks and open relationships. If you forget that, you can forget everything.

A TEAM VICTORY ACCOMPLISHED WITHOUT JEALOUSY

Moving forward a couple of chapters in the Book of Joshua, we come to another scene entirely, and a completely different strategy. This time its not Jericho, it's a place named Ai. The plan is an ambush.

> Now the Lord said to Joshua, "Do not fear or be dismayed. Take all the people of war with you and arise, go up to Ai; see, I have given into your hand the king of Ai, his people, his city, and his land.
> "And you shall do to Ai and its king just as you did to Jericho and its king; you shall take only its spoil and its cattle as plunder for yourselves. Set an ambush for the city behind it."
> So Joshua rose with all the people of war to go up to Ai; and Joshua chose 30,000 men, valiant warriors, and sent them out at night.

And he commanded them, saying, "See, you are going to ambush the city from behind it. Do not go very far from the city,
but all of you be ready.

"Then I and all the people who are with me will approach
the city. And it will come about when they come out to meet
us as at the first, that we will flee before them.

"And they will come out after us until we have drawn them
away from the city, for they will say, 'They are fleeing before us
as at the first.' So we will flee before them.

"And you shall rise from your ambush and take possession of
the city, for the Lord your God will deliver it into your hand.

"Then it will be when you have seized the city, that you shall
set the city on fire. You shall do it according to the word of
the Lord. See, I have commanded you."

So Joshua sent them away, and they went to the place of ambush
and remained between Bethel and Ai, on the west side of Ai;
but Joshua spent that night among the people (Josh. 8:1–9).

Get the picture? Again, it's not complicated. Different people
were to do different jobs. Some were up front with Joshua, others
would be away from the glory. It didn't matter to them because
they were committed to a team victory, regardless. Nobody asked,
"Now, who gets the credit?" Or "Do I have to be one of those
out of the limelight?" No, a unified team spirit has no room
for that.

So they stationed the people, all the army that was on the
north side of the city, and its rear guard on the west side of the
city, and Joshua spent that night in the midst of the valley.

And it came about when the king of Ai saw it, that the men
of the city hurried and rose up early and went out to meet Israel
in battle, he and all his people at the appointed place before
the desert plain. But he did not know that there was an ambush
against him behind the city.

And Joshua and all Israel pretended to be beaten before them,
and fled by the way of the wilderness.

And all the people who were in the city were called together
to pursue them, and they pursued Joshua, and were drawn away
from the city.

So not a man was left in Ai or Bethel who had not gone out after Israel, and they left the city unguarded and pursued Israel.

And the men in ambush rose quickly from their place, and when he had stretched out his hand, they ran and entered the city and captured it; and they quickly set the city on fire.

When the men of Ai turned back and looked, behold, the smoke of the city ascended to the sky, and they had no place to flee this way or that, for the people who had been fleeing to the wilderness turned against the pursuers.

When Joshua and all Israel saw that the men in ambush had captured the city and that the smoke of the city ascended, they turned back and slew the men of Ai (Josh. 8:13–17, 19–21).

How interesting! There was no argument, no struggle among the troops to be a javelin assistant or the lead man in the rear guard, no competition. True humility prevailed among everyone on the team, including the star players.

I was thumbing through one of the national periodicals recently and happened upon a picture of President Reagan sitting in the Oval Office. He was behind his desk, signing some document as others were standing on either side. I noticed a small sign on his desk that was too small to read. It intrigued me. I found a magnifying glass and looked closer; the print was blurred, but I could read enough of the sign to know it was worth the effort to pursue. The next morning I had my secretary telephone the White House and talk with someone who could give us the information we wanted. It was well worth the effort. The sign on President Reagan's desk says:

**THERE IS NO LIMIT TO WHAT A MAN CAN DO
OR WHERE HE CAN GO IF HE DOESN'T MIND
WHO GETS THE CREDIT.**

The ancient Hebrews didn't have such a sign, but they practiced its truth. They won the victory at Ai because each person was willing to be absorbed in the plan, regardless of who got the credit.

This reminds me of something Dietrich Bonhoeffer once wrote. See if you don't find it insightful and penetrating.

"There arose a reasoning among them, which of them should be the greatest" (Luke 9:46). We know who it is that sows this thought in the Christian community. But perhaps we do not bear in mind enough that no Christian community ever comes together without this thought immediately emerging as a seed of discord. Thus at the very beginning of Christian fellowship there is engendered an invisible, often unconscious, life-and-death contest. "There arose a reasoning among them": this is enough to destroy a fellowship.

Hence it is vitally necessary that every Christian community from the very outset face this dangerous enemy squarely, and eradicate it. There is no time to lose here, for from the first moment when a man meets another person he is looking for a strategic position he can assume and hold over against that person. There are strong persons and weak ones. If a man is not strong, he immediately claims the right of the weak as his own and uses it against the strong. There are gifted and ungifted persons, simple people and difficult people, devout and less devout, the sociable and the solitary. Does not the ungifted person have to take up a position just as well as the gifted person, the difficult one as well as the simple? And if I am not gifted, then perhaps I am devout anyhow; or if I am not devout it is only because I do not want to be. May not the sociable individual carry the field before him and put the timid, solitary man to shame? Then may not the solitary person become the undying enemy and ultimate vanquisher of his sociable adversary? Where is there a person who does not with instinctive sureness find the spot where he can stand and defend himself, but which he will never give up to another, for which he will fight with all the drive of his instinct of self-assertion?

All this can occur in the most polite or even pious environment. But the important thing is that a Christian community should know that somewhere in it there will certainly be "a reasoning among them, which of them should be the greatest." It is the struggle of the natural man for self-justification. He finds it only in comparing himself with others, in condemning and judging others. . . .

[When the Christian community eradicates this enemy] strong and weak, wise and foolish, gifted or ungifted, pious or impious, the diverse individuals in the community, are no longer incentives for talking and judging and condemning, and thus excuses for self-justification. They are rather cause for rejoicing in one another and serving one another.[2]

A TRUST IN GOD CLAIMED WITHOUT DOUBT

Faced with battle fatigue, the Hebrews realized that unless the Lord intervened, they would never make it. Exhausted, they needed divine strength to carry on.

> Then the men of Gibeon sent word to Joshua to the camp at Gilgal, saying, "Do not abandon your servants; come up to us quickly and save us and help us, for all the kings of the Amorites that live in the hill country have assembled against us."
>
> So Joshua went up from Gilgal, he and all the people of war with him and all the valiant warriors.
>
> And the Lord said to Joshua, "Do not fear them, for I have given them into your hands; not one of them shall stand before you."
>
> So Joshua came upon them suddenly by marching all night from Gilgal (Josh. 10:6–9).

During my days in the Marines, I remember a nonstop march that lasted for about four hours—but *never* all night. I cannot imagine how exhausted Joshua and his fighting men must have been. They really needed God to step in and supplement their weakness with His strength. And did He ever! He did a never-to-be-repeated miracle.

> And the Lord confounded them before Israel, and He slew them with a great slaughter at Gibeon, and pursued them by the way of the ascent of Beth-horon, and struck them as far as Azekah and Makkedah.
>
> And it came about as they fled from before Israel, while they were at the descent of Beth-horon, that the Lord threw large

stones from heaven on them as far as Azekah, and they died; there were more who died from the hailstones than those whom the sons of Israel killed with the sword.

Then Joshua spoke to the Lord in the day when the Lord delivered up the Amorites before the sons of Israel, and he said in the sight of Israel,

"O sun, stand still at Gibeon,
And O moon in the valley of Aijalon."
So the sun stood still, and the moon stopped.
Until the nation avenged themselves of their enemies.

Is it not written in the book of Jashar? And the sun stopped in the middle of the sky, and did not hasten to go down for about a whole day.

And there was no day like that before it or after it, when the Lord listened to the voice of a man; for the Lord fought for Israel (Josh. 10:10–14).

There's one for *That's Incredible!* Can't you see it? By now, feeling confident in God, General Joshua looks up and shouts, "Sun, stop!" And then, "Moon, you too!" Don't view the man as presumptuous. No, it's not that. It's the realization that God is very much involved in one's motive and totally glorified in one's actions. It's like Theodore Epp has written: "Once a man is satisfied that he is in the center of God's plan and God is working out His will through him, that man is invincible."[3]

You can read the results for yourself in Joshua 10:11–27. The territory was successfully invaded, the kings were captured and killed, and God was glorified. Such was the result of a team of dedicated warriors who were committed to unity, who willingly became examples of humility and determined to believe God, regardless.

SOME SUGGESTIONS FOR APPLICATION

How easy it is to leave all these great accounts riveted to ancient history. And how wrong to do so! Here are a couple of thoughts worth our time and consideration.

1. *The pursuit of unity is hard work, but it's worth it.*

If you are in a Christian leadership role, you are commanded to "preserve the unity of the Spirit in the bond of peace" (Eph. 4:3). There will be every temptation *not* to do that. Others around you will encourage you to choose sides or stand against certain people rather than finding ways to stand with them. You'll be tempted to manipulate or control or in some other way gain mastery over others . . . and for one reason—to get your way, to massage your own pride.

I suggest you be different. Commit yourself to freeing others so they can grow and discover on their own. For a change, as much as is possible, walk away from an argument rather than inviting one. Become more of a peacemaker.

You may have heard the story; nevertheless, I find folks smile every time I tell it. A man and his wife were married for over fifty years. Someone asked the gentleman the secret of their marital bliss. "Well," the old man drawled, "the wife and I had this agreement when we first got married. It went like this: When she was bothered about somethin', she'd jus' tell me an git it off her chest. And if I was mad at her about somethin', I was to take a long walk. I s'ppose you could attribute our happy marriage to the fact that I have largely led an outdoor life."

Now *there's* a guy committed to unity. It will not come easily, but it's worth every effort, believe me. That brings us to my next thought for consideration.

2. *The place of humility is of highest value, but it's rarely seen.*

By now you realize how closely unity and humility are tied together. One breeds the other; neither can exist without the other. They're like Siamese twins, perpetually connected. Personally, I have seen numerous occasions when pride won out (even though it was never called that) and harmony faded away . . . and I mean fast. It's like James says, "What is the source of quarrels and conflicts among you? Is not the source your pleasures that wage war in your members? You lust and do not have; so you commit murder. And you are envious and cannot obtain; so you fight and quarrel" (James 4:1–2).

Contrary to the stuff you might read today, the words, *fight* and *quarrel*, are not apt descriptions of the way to get ahead. They won't ultimately glorify God. Friends are made by *not* fighting and by *refusing* to quarrel.

I've appreciated the wise words of Alan McGinnis so much. In his fine little book, *The Friendship Factor*, he addresses this head on.

> Pop psychology has produced a new wave of self-help books that advocate asserting yourself, doing your own thing, taking advantage of the other person before the other person takes advantage of you, and telling anyone who does not give you what you "need" in your relationship to get lost. Actually, the movement is not entirely new. Arrogance has been around for some time.
>
> But there is a pathos to such a philosophy. It is the attempt of unhappy people to find some joy for themselves. Someone has told them that they will find it by ignoring the needs and wants of people around them and elbowing their way to the front of the line. But my experience in counseling such people is that when they push others away, intimidate their competitors, and disregard those to whom they have responsibility, they get to the front of the line and discover that there is no one there to hand them anything. Jesus dismissed such a life-style, saying that those who save their lives will end up losing them.
>
> Christ also said that those who lose their lives will save them, and the Bible is replete with statements to the effect that sacrificing ourselves and denying ourselves for some higher good will in the long run bring happiness. In other words, happiness does not ordinarily come to those who set out to "be happy." Happiness is more often a by-product.
>
> I notice that the happiest people do not have to shove and push. They do not worry about intimidating others; they are confident of their own self-worth, much of which comes from making other people happy. There are rewards for such acts, for the friend who is willing to sacrifice for you is not easily forgotten.[4]

David's song lives on. Although he composed it centuries ago, long before books like *Pulling Your Own Strings* or *Looking*

Out for #1 made the bestseller list, it is still true. Listen to the lyrics once again:

> How good and pleasant it is
>   when brothers live together in unity!
> It is like precious oil poured on the head,
>   running down on the beard. . . .

Want some good counsel? Spread a little oil around. Don't be too careful. Pour it out. Let it splash and run down. Start today.

DISCUSSION IDEAS AND QUESTIONS

- Define unity in your own words. Be a little creative. Add some thoughts that embellish your definition.
- Why are we, by nature, rigid rather than free? Why are we more narrow than open?
- Go back to Jesus' prayer in John 17:20–26. Analyze it in light of today's push for independence and intimidation. Name one way you could be more committed to unity.
- Discuss the need for affirmation. Can you recall a time when someone affirmed you and it renewed your spirit? Share it.
- Talk openly about the acid of jealousy. Is this one of your battles? Or have you been the brunt of someone's jealous assault? How can jealousy be conquered?
- Go back and read again the words of Dietrich Bonhoeffer. Discuss his remarks concerning the strong and the weak.
- Finally, take time to think through the two principles on unity and humility. Why are they so closely connected? Read Philippians 2:3–4. Talk about how that applies to you today.

6

When the Fellowship
Breaks Down

It's TIME FOR A big dose of reality. So far things seem fairly
smooth. You may have thought a little bit about disharmony
and periodic conflicts, but for the most part, you could begin
to get the impression that open relationships and vulnerability
are like a downhill slide. With your rose-colored glasses in
place, you might even start believing that fellow members of
the body invariably pull together as they get closer. You may
be on the verge of thinking that once you unmask and deal
honestly with others, an uninterrupted path of peace will be
yours to enjoy. It ain't necessarily so! Occasionally, mutiny
occurs among the body members, and the results can be devas-
tating.

As I read the following words of a surgeon describing the
presence of cancer in a human body, I thought of how vividly
his description fit the family of God when there is a breakdown
in our fellowship.

A tumor is called benign if its effect is fairly localized and it stays within membrane boundaries. But the most traumatizing condition in the body occurs when disloyal cells defy inhibition. They multiply without any checks on growth, spreading rapidly throughout the body, choking out normal cells. White cells, armed against foreign invaders, will not attack the body's own mutinous cells. Physicians fear no other malfunction more deeply: it is called cancer. For still mysterious reasons, these cells—and they may be tissues—grow wild, out of control. Each is a healthy, functioning cell, but disloyal, no longer acting in regard for the rest of the body.

Even the white cells, the dependable palace guard, can destroy the body through rebellion. Sometimes they recklessly reproduce, clogging the bloodstream, overloading the lymph system, strangling the body's normal functions—such is leukemia.[1]

And such is the spiritual disease called relational conflicts. When the fellowship breaks down, the fun stops and the body aches. How damaging those times can be!

They are certainly not new. The path of the church is strewn with the litter of conflict, disagreement, friction, in-fighting, and discord. Just think back to the church in the first century as you mentally stroll through the book of Acts.

- Acts 5: Hypocrisy resulting in divine discipline.
- Acts 6: Unfair treatment of minorities and the needy.
- Acts 9: Resistance to allow Paul, a recent convert, to minister.
- Acts 11: Legalism rears its ugly head.
- Acts 15: Doctrinal disagreement so strong that an official council was needed to settle the issue. And toward the end of the same chapter, a personal clash between Paul and Barnabas occurred.

Neither time nor space permit me to trace the scene of conflict from then until now (that would take multiple volumes), but there is sufficient evidence to prove that this mighty army, the

Church of God, has never been completely free of conflict or crisis.

It may be as severe and explosive as the time of the Inquisition when Christians were killed by church officials who thought they were doing God a favor. Or it may be as mild and common-place as a Sunday school teacher unable to control a class of preteens.

Leadership magazine, known for its choice cartoons about the church, made all of us smile with understanding as this particular scene pictured a grim-faced preacher pausing during his sermon delivery and reading a note that said: "We interrupt this sermon to inform you that the fourth-grade boys are now in complete control of their Sunday school class and are holding Miss Moseby hostage."[2]

REASONS FELLOWSHIP BREAKS DOWN

Since conflicts do occur, since the fellowship does break down, it seems only right that we face it head on. Let's begin by looking at the big picture. When are the times people pull away and resist assimilation? When are we especially prone to be isolated and keep our masks securely in place? I can think of at least five times, and each one is illustrated in biblical accounts.

Extreme Suffering and Sickness

Given enough pain, most of us will seek to be alone. Whether it be physical or emotional pain, few are the sufferers who remain in the mainstream of involvement. The reasons are many. We can be embarrassed by what we are struggling with. Or we can be so broken and bruised within that depression pulls us aside. Obviously, if we are enduring a physical illness that saps our strength or requires long days of bedrest, we're simply unable to stay up with life's demands.

Job fell victim to a dread bodily disease—boils all over his body. You'll recall that he sat *alone* in his misery (Job 1:20–

ALDERSGATE COLLEGE
LIBRARY

21; 2:7–13). Even when his alleged "friends" came to comfort
him (*confront* is a better description), Job stayed away from
his normal responsibilities. Pain does that to us. If it endures
long enough and hits us hard enough, we opt for isolation. Like
Job, we often prefer to be outside the gaze of the inquisitive.

King Saul did too. Remember, he sat all alone in the darkness
of his despair submerged in the swamp of depression (1 Sam.
15–16).

Our Savior also sought to be alone when the agony of the
cross began to take its toll on Him (Matt. 26:36–44). We should
not be surprised or offended, therefore, when others, today, remove themselves from involvement due to pain. On the contrary,
a sensitive understanding heart of compassion is our best response. However, when we reach out to them it must be with
utmost tact and sensitivity. I'll address that subject at length
in chapter 8.

Burnout and Fatigue

In this day of great pressure, high stress, constant demands,
and little leisure, more and more of God's people are dropping
through the cracks as victims of burnout and fatigue. It is not
uncommon to meet those in the Lord's business who have worked
themselves into a frenzy, burning the proverbial candle at both
ends until there is neither candle nor wick left to burn. They
find themselves weary and dreary souls greatly in need of rest—
time to repair and heal—not at all interested in programs or
projects that require energy and more time. Those folks need
to be respected, not harrassed. They need time to work through
and silence "the tyranny of the urgent."

Dear old Elijah would say a resounding "Amen." From the
frying pan of intense involvement as God's prophet, who stood
alone against King Ahab and his wife Jezebel, into the fire on
Mount Carmel as he faced the prophets of Baal, Elijah was in
the thick of it for years (if you include the time he endured
the lengthy drought). He had prayed, prophesied, fought,
preached, suffered, confronted the king, and mocked the false

prophets. Suddenly, his equilibrium snapped as he stumbled into the wilderness all alone and begged Jehovah to take his life (1 Kings 19:1–5). Burned out and fatigued, the prophet was finished and famished. His vision of the big picture was blurred and his motivation for ministry had vanished. It is beautiful to study how graciously God dealt with His man. No guilt trip. No long sermon. Not even a frown or a threat. With divine compassion He allowed the prophet time to repair, and He gave him space to recover. He even catered a meal for the exhausted prophet to enjoy. All of us could learn much from God's therapy.

Periodically, we'll have folks slip into our church who are in need of inner healing. They are spent. Hungry for a place to repair, they long for the freedom to be still and to gain renewed perspective. Such folks are to be respected and allowed some room to recover. They don't need somebody to corner them and "put 'em to work." In such cases, assimilation and involvement need to be put on hold. Their greater need (as in the case of Elijah) is to be allowed the freedom to relax. In due time, the energy and perspective will return. Burnout isn't a terminal disease in most cases.

Trouble at Home or Personal Turmoil

Shame is often added to pain when trouble at home or inner personal turmoil sends us running for cover. Who can describe the intense anxiety connected with domestic conflicts or financial reversal or moral compromise? Any number of such dilemmas create within us a desire to be isolated even though that may not be the best course of action.

David, while guilty of the affair with Bathsheba, was not engaged in his normal high-level standard of responsibilities. Read 2 Samuel 11 and 12 and Psalm 32:3–5 and Psalm 51:1–17 for yourself. They give us sufficient reason to believe that during those dark days, he wrote no songs, he fought no war, he made no significant decisions. Rather, he was caught in his self-made web, removed and preoccupied. Whipped by guilt, he hurt alone.

The same can occur when a family struggles with a rebellious teenager or young adult. This kind of problem can sap a family's strength and steal their joy. Such folks usually isolate themselves and walk through that dismal valley alone.

As a pastor I often find myself impaled on the horns of a dilemma. Should I step in? Should I "intrude" and offer my assistance, even though uninvited? Or should I stay out of the way and let the individuals involved work through the conflict themselves? There are no hard-and-fast rules. I've done both . . . and had both *backfire!* I have also had both result in a wonderful healing and recovery. In my head I can still hear both extremes:

"What business is this of yours? If you had stayed out of it, we could've worked things out."

And:

"Thank you. Thank you! Had you not stepped in and cared enough to comfort (or confront or listen—whatever), who knows where we'd be today?"

And:

"We appreciate the fact that you gave us room to work through the conflict. Thank you for not pushing your way in and forcing the issue."

And:

"Where were you? Why didn't you make yourself available? Obviously, you didn't care even though you knew we were hurting."

It's enough to make an isolationist out of a preacher. Wouldn't it be helpful to have fail-safe rules to follow on certain supersensitive occasions? But when the fellowship breaks down, black and white rule books need to be tossed into the sea. And people who tend to follow them should take a hike.

Friction between Two or More Individuals

Another barrier to involvement and unguarded relationships is the familiar problem of people-with-people conflicts—personality clashes, disagreement with another's decision, offenses that lack closure and full forgiveness, misunderstandings that get complicated by rumor and gossip. This is *especially* so if the person who is isolated and licking his wounds got hurt because he or she reached out to another in sincerity and got burned in the process.

I often call to mind the words of Solomon: "A brother offended is harder to be won than a strong city, and contentions are like the bars of a castle" (Prov. 18:19).

Can you picture it? Thick, rusty, foreboding bars that say, "Stay away from me! I want to be left alone." But if you track the analogy to its limit, you see that it's the offended one who suffers the most. He is the person who shuts himself off and steps out of circulation. How bitter one can become behind those invisible bars.

> A story is told of two unmarried sisters who had so bitter a ruckus they stopped speaking to each other. Unable or unwilling to leave their small home, they continued to use the same rooms and sleep in the same bedroom. A chalk line divided the sleeping area into two halves, separating doorway and fireplace, so that each could come and go and get her own meals without trespassing on her sister's domain. In the black of night each could hear the breathing of the foe. For years they co-existed in grinding silence. Neither was willing to take the first step to reconciliation.[3]

How much better to follow the model of two other unmarried sisters, Betsy and Corrie ten Boom. In Corrie's book, *The Hiding Place*, she mentions seeing Betsy's face swollen and bruised. Corrie asked her if she had been beaten by the guard. Her sister's answer amazed Corrie. Betsy said, "I felt sorry for that man." Who knows how many of us frequently call to mind the forgiving spirit of Corrie ten Boom, which she learned from her sister?

Paul and Barnabas had a face-off, according to Acts 15:36–40. Two mature, strong, determined men disagreed and parted company. Each was so convinced he was right that he was willing to end a relationship because of an inner conviction. We read nothing more of Barnabas as he slipped away to Cyprus following that sharp disagreement.

How unusual we are! If we have trouble with our car, we don't give up driving. If we have a roof that leaks, we don't abandon the house and move to another place. But the irony of it all is that when a couple of folks have a conflict, only rarely are they big enough to stay at it and work things out. More often, they walk away and live lives of quiet desperation. If antiques are worth the time and energy and expense involved in restoring, so are broken relationships.

Open Disobedience against God

This is a category I'd like to explore in greater depth, since it is illustrated so clearly in the narrative of the ancient Hebrews, which we have been following.

Simply stated, this is a subject that has to do with the isolation that comes as a direct consequence of disobedience. How easy it is to pull away from God's people and live the rest of our days in seclusion because we once blew it royally and suffered because of it. Since we're His children, God disciplines us for our disobedience, not so we'll spend the rest of our lives in isolation, but that we might learn the value of walking in obedience.

For a classic example look at what happened when certain Hebrews were disobedient at Ai.

AI AND THE HEBREWS

The book of Joshua is sort of an *Indianapolis 500* of the Old Testament. Racing from one battle to another, those Hebrews set new records for speed in triumph. With hardly a moment's hesitation, they swept through Jericho, driving a wedge into the central section of Canaan and weakening the enemy's defense. Then they pressed on to other challenges, ready to handle whatever opponent they might encounter . . . until Ai.

Joshua 7 is the pit stop. Everything suddenly screeches to a halt. The driver (Joshua) sits there confused, wondering to himself, "What happened? Why the problem? What's wrong?" Not even his crew could figure it out.

You need to understand that, militarily, Ai was a pushover. Compared to formidable Jericho, it was a "hole in the road," a clod of dirt on the road to victory. But the Israeli army was soundly whipped . . . blown away by a bunch of rednecks from a country town in Canaan.

> Now Joshua sent men from Jericho to Ai, which is near Beth-aven, east of Bethel, and said to them, "Go up and spy out the land." So the men went up and spied out Ai.
>
> And they returned to Joshua and said to him, "Do not let all the people go up; only about two or three thousand men need go up to Ai; do not make all the people toil up there, for they are few."
>
> So about three thousand men from the people went up there, but they fled from the men of Ai.
>
> And the men of Ai struck down about thirty-six of their men, and pursued them from the gate as far as Shebarium, and struck them down on the descent, so the hearts of the people melted and became as water (Josh. 7:2–5).

Let's understand that we're not interested in merely studying ancient history. Our goal is to gain insight and reproof as God teaches us from these Old Testament scriptures. Neither are we concerned about all the details of military strategy. We're thinking about relationships in this book and, particularly in this chapter, why and how those relationships break down. In light of that, the first step in dealing with a broken relationship is an awareness that something is different, something is wrong. Actually, there are four stages we must work through in restoring relationships.

Stage One: "Something Is Wrong"

We'll call this the "symptom stage." As I study the Ai battle, I find a couple of things out of whack. First, there was a break-

down in the normal routine—the Hebrews encountered an opposite reaction from what they expected. Instead of a slight skir-
mish, there was wholesale resistance. Instead of the enemy's
being little more than a corporal's guard, they became an impos-
ing body of warriors. The normal routine was disrupted. Second,
there was discouragement and a loss of morale as the Hebrews'
"hearts . . . melted and became as water" (v. 5).

In relationships that begin to break down, the "symptom
stage" takes on a similar setting. We notice first an alteration
in routine. The person no longer comes around. Or when he
or she does come, there are strained feelings—awkwardness, lack
of eye contact, a rush to leave. There is no longer the free-
flowing give-and-take in conversation. The sense of humor is
decidedly absent. Things are definitely different. "Something
is wrong," we whisper to ourselves.

Also, to use the words from verse 5, your heart "melts" within
you. You churn. Deep within your spirit you feel a distance, a
space that once was not there. By the way, the more sensitive
you are toward people, the quicker you detect such symptoms.
You feel "bad vibes" as you encounter one another.

This leads to the "concern stage."

Stage Two: "What Has Happened?"

Go back with me to the battle scene at Ai. Imagine yourself
in Joshua's place as you read these words:

> Then Joshua tore his clothes and fell to the earth on his face
> before the ark of the Lord until the evening, both he and the
> elders of Israel; and they put dust on their heads.
> And Joshua said, "Alas, O Lord God, why didst Thou ever
> bring this people over the Jordan, only to deliver us into the
> hand of the Amorites, to destroy us? If only we had been willing
> to dwell beyond the Jordan!
> "Oh Lord, what can I say since Israel has turned their back
> before their enemies?
> "For the Canaanites and all the inhabitants of the land will

hear of it, and they will surround us and cut off our name from the earth. And what wilt Thou do for Thy great name?" (Josh. 7:6–9).

There is confusion. The man is naturally concerned about the strange twist of events. He gets together wih his most trusted friends (called "elders"—v. 6), and they seek God's mind for wisdom. Those men are serious as they pray and as they enter into this concern together. The confusion drives them to their knees.

We do the same, don't we? Having felt the distance between us and the other person, we talk it over and pray with a few very close—and I should add very *confidential*—friends. Through times in prayer, we gain insight. God gives us the ability to penetrate the surface.

I have a few very close and confidential friends. They are so important to me that you may have noticed I dedicated this book to each one of them. These men hold our relationship in highest regard and great trust. They view our times together (as I do) as exceedingly important occasions. We talk. We think. We evaluate decisions. We share our struggles. We pray. We invest these hours with the realization that God uses us in each other's lives. We are available and we are in touch. Our goal is to strengthen and help one another any way we can. By being accountable and vulnerable in our times together, we are able to get to the heart of the issue without the standard smoke screens and fog that frequently cloud friendships. I rather suspect that Joshua had something like this going with the men who shared his burden.

The Lord honored their pursuit as He broke the silence and unveiled the mystery.

So the Lord said to Joshua, "Rise up! Why is it that you have fallen on your face?

"Israel has sinned, and they have also transgressed My covenant which I commanded them. And they have even taken some of the things under the ban and have both stolen and deceived.

Moreover, they have also put them among their own things.

"Therefore the sons of Israel cannot stand before their enemies; they turn their backs before their enemies, for they have become accursed, I will not be with you any more unless you destroy the things under the ban from your midst.

"Rise up! Consecrate the people and say, 'Consecrate yourselves for tomorrow, for thus the Lord, the God of Israel, has said, "There are things under the ban in your midst, O Israel. You cannot stand before your enemies until you have removed the things under the ban from your midst."

'In the morning then you shall come near by your tribes. And it shall be that the tribe which the Lord takes by lot shall come near by families, and the family which the Lord takes shall come near by households, and the household which the Lord takes shall come near man by man.

'And it shall be that the one who is taken with the things under the ban shall be burned with fire, he and all that belongs to him, because he has transgressed the covenant of the Lord, and because he has committed a disgraceful thing in Israel' " (Josh. 7:10-15).

Jehovah didn't reveal *everything,* but He certainly made it clear that disobedience was on the loose among the Israeli army. Someone was guilty of transgression. Names weren't revealed, but the disease was found. Perhaps it would help to go back and read about the "ban" God had placed on His people as they invaded Canaan.

"But as for you, only keep yourselves from the things under the ban lest you covet them and take some of the things under the ban, so you would make the camp of Israel accursed and bring trouble on it.

"But all the silver and gold and articles of bronze and iron are holy to the Lord; they shall go into the treasury of the Lord" (Josh. 6:18-19).

Because someone had willfully and deliberately broken with God's directive, defeat had entered the ranks of that otherwise victorious army. Now it was time to discover that person. The "discovery stage" is next.

Stage Three: "Who Is Involved?"

Through a careful probing process of analysis, Joshua seeks to determine the source.

> So Joshua arose early in the morning and brought Israel near by tribes, and the tribe of Judah was taken.
>
> And he brought the family of Judah near, and he took the family of the Zerahites; and he brought the family of the Zerahites near man by man, and Zabdi was taken.
>
> And he brought his household near man by man; and Achan, son of Carmi, son of Zabdi, son of Zerah, from the tribe of Judah, was taken.
>
> Then Joshua said to Achan, "My son, I implore you, give glory to the Lord, the God of Israel, and give praise to Him; and tell me now what you have done. Do not hide it from me."
>
> So Achan answered Joshua and said, "Truly, I have sinned against the Lord, the God of Israel, and this is what I did; when I saw among the spoil a beautiful mantle from Shinar and two hundred shekels of silver and a bar of gold fifty shekels in weight, then I coveted them and took them; and behold, they are concealed in the earth inside my tent with the silver underneath it" (Josh. 7:16–21).

Great effort was expended. Confrontation followed. The commander didn't jump to conclusions or put words in the guilty party's mouth. He listened. He was willing to hear him out, to let the whole thing be confessed. He invited the whole truth, "Do not hide it from me" (v. 19).

This is not at all enjoyable. It doesn't come easily and it is often not by invitation. If the fellowship has broken down because of open disobedience against God (as in this case with Achan), the confrontation is usually painful and tearful. So it is important that things be done in the right spirit. I will go so far as to say if you enjoy such encounters, you have the wrong motive. Paul writes wise words:

> Brothers, if someone is caught in a sin, you who are spiritual should restore him gently. But watch yourself, or you also may

be tempted. Carry each other's burdens, and in this way you will fulfill the law of Christ (Gal. 6:1–2, NIV).

James adds:

> My brothers, if any of you should wander away from the truth and another should turn him back on to the right path, then the latter may be sure that in turning a man back from his wandering course he has rescued a soul from death, and his loving action will "cover a multitude of sins" (James 5:19–20, PHILLIPS).

These times of discovery, confrontation, and confession among fellow Christians are not to be carried out in the courtroom of law (1 Cor. 6:4–8), nor are they to be pushed in front of a church congregation unless *every* effort toward reconciliation has been tried and met with resistance (Matt. 18:15–17). I repeat, the spirit in which we go about such painful times is as important as the actions themselves, sometimes more so.

Invariably, this leads to the "assistance stage."

Stage Four: "What Is Needed?"

In the case of Achan, there was no alternative. God had spoken. His law had been broken. Death was the required penalty in that era under the Mosaic Law. Joshua did not hesitate. Maximum punishment was carried out. The people never forgot the scene.

> So Joshua sent messengers, and they ran to the tent; and behold, it was concealed in his tent with the silver underneath it.
>
> And they took them from inside the tent and brought them to Joshua and to all the sons of Israel, and they poured them out before the Lord.
>
> Then Joshua and all Israel with him, took Achan the son of Zerah, the silver, the mantle, the bar of gold, his sons, his daughters, his oxen, his donkeys, his sheep, his tent and all that belonged to him; and they brought them up to the valley of Achor.

And Joshua said, "Why have you troubled us? The Lord will trouble you this day." And all Israel stoned them with stones; and they burned them with fire after they had stoned them with stones.

And they raised over him a great heap of stones that stands to this day, and the Lord turned from the fierceness of His anger. Therefore the name of that place has been called the Valley of Achor to this day (Josh. 7:22–26).

In our day, an era of mercy and grace, we are occasionally the instruments of judgment. This is never a pleasant role to fill, but nevertheless, it is an essential one. The full recovery of a brother or sister in God's family often depends on our willingness to step in and assist the person to face and admit the truth, then, hopefully, reach full repentance.

Nathan was God's instrument of confrontation in David's life. Had he not gone to the adulterous king and looked him squarely in the eye and said, "You are the man!" who knows how much longer David would have lingered in sin? Who can tell how many more people would have suffered in the fallout of his transgression?

On several occasions it has fallen my lot to be the Nathan in someone's life. I have *never* enjoyed that role, I can assure you. More often I have begged the Lord to have someone else do the dirty work. But after the whole episode has ended in confession and repentance, I have been grateful to God for His giving me the courage to step in and help a brother or sister come to terms with the things they were refusing to face. Sometimes, like it or not, it is necessary to blast before we can build.

Let me repeat something to make it so clear that no one will misunderstand. Not all breakdowns in fellowship call for confrontation and direct intervention. In the case of open disobedience against God where the Lord's family and His name are suffering (as was clearly the case with Achan at Ai), those drastic measures must be taken . . . yet even then, the *way* they are done is as important as *that* they are done.

Ai and Me

Three lasting principles linger as we draw this chapter to a close.

- Most fellowship breakdowns that are the result of open disobedience against God will not heal themselves. GET INVOLVED.
- The longer the breakdown, the greater the impact. START TODAY.
- Solutions will be initially painful but ultimately rewarding. DON'T QUIT.

Let me ask you, if you had a tumor and your doctor, having examined you, had determined that it was malignant, would you want him to ignore telling you the hard truth? Would he be a friend and a competent professional if he acted as though everything were great and that you had nothing to be concerned about? Would you recommend him to others?

If we want the truth from those who keep watch over our physical condition, how much more we should want the truth from those who keep watch over our souls.

Painful, thankless, and grim though it may be, telling our brothers and sisters the truth—in love—is still one of the most important functions we can carry out in the body of Christ. May God give us the courage to keep doing so . . . for the sake of keeping His body healthy . . . and that occasionally calls for a big dose of reality.

DISCUSSION IDEAS AND QUESTIONS

- Think about the family of God as a body made up of many parts. Think of a breakdown in the body as a disease. What are some things we can do to help keep the body healthy so that disease doesn't invade?
- Looking back over the various reasons fellowship breaks down, discuss each one briefly. Can you think of someone who might be drifting today because of one of these problems? Without calling their name, consider ways you could reach out and be a healing agent.
- A term we sometimes hear these days is "wounded healer." Someone who has been broken or bruised through previous pain ("wounded") is often the best instrument for helping others recover ("healer"). Talk about why this is true.
- Achan's sin had a tremendous impact on the entire Hebrew army. Are there times when *our* transgressions have a similar impact on the broader body of Christ?
- Read Galatians 6:1–2 and James 5:19–20. As you meditate on these verses, talk about the importance of going with the right spirit to those who have been ensnared by sin. Address the importance of humility.
- Turn to 1 Corinthians 10:12. What does it say to you about this matter of confrontation?
- Are you close to at least one other person, preferably several? Is that relationship open and unguarded so that others have the freedom to say the hard thing to you, if necessary? Describe how you have cultivated this intimacy. Give God thanks for the gift of friendship.

7

Authentic
Love

HAL DAVID AND BURT BACHARACH are familiar names to music lovers all over America. What Rogers and Hammerstein were in the '40s and '50s, David and Bacharach were in the '60s and '70s.

The former did the lyrics and the latter wrote the melodies to such well-known pieces as "I Say a Little Prayer for You." and "Close to You" and "One Less Bell to Answer" . . . and, of course, the Academy Award-winning "Raindrops Keep Fallin' on My Head."

But, of all their music, the single tune that won our country's heart more than any other was the one that sang its way into our loneliness and hunger for love.

> What the world needs now is love, sweet love,
> No—not just for some but for everyone;
> Lord, we don't need another mountain,

There are mountains and hillsides enough to climb,
There are oceans and rivers enough to cross . . .
Enough to last 'til the end of time.

What the world needs now is love, sweet love;
No—not just for some, but for everyone
It's the only thing that there's just too little of.[1]

Do you believe that? Probably so. But the world doesn't need phony love; or mushy, fickle, wimpy love; or conditional love that says "if you ———, then I'll love you;" or swap-meet love that says "Because you gave me this, I'll swap you love in return." No. What the world needs now is tough love, *authentic* love.

That's the stuff open relationships are all about. It's *that* kind of love that makes me care enough to confront and big enough to forgive. David and Bacharach were exactly right, this rare commodity is "the only thing there's just too little of."

A CASE OF AUTHENTIC LOVE

Gayle Sayers was the best running back the Chicago Bears ever had. He was black. Brian Piccolo was the other running back, also quite an athlete. He was white. This was nothing new, not even back in 1967. Blacks and whites often played on the same professional teams. But these two were different. They were roommates on the road—a first for race relations in professional football. You need to realize that Sayers had never had a close relationship with *any* white man, with the exception, perhaps, of George Halas, the head coach of the Bears. And Piccolo admitted he had never *known* a black person—not really.

But within the span of two brief years, 1967–1969, their relationship had deepened into one of the most memorable friendships in the history of sports. As the movie *Brian's Song* poignantly depicted, the men truly *loved* each other. Part of the reason they grew so close together was the tragic fact that

Brian Piccolo contracted cancer during the 1969 season. Although he fought to play the season out, he was in the hospital more than he was on the playing field. Frequently, Sayers flew to be beside his friend as the disease refused to go away. The smell of death became increasingly more obvious though the two of them, both winners through and through, refused to surrender.

They and their wives had longstanding plans to sit together at the annual Professional Football Writers' Banquet in New York where Gayle Sayers, appropriately, was to receive the George S. Halas award as "the most courageous player in professional football." By the time of the banquet, Piccolo was too sick to attend. He was confined to his bed at home.

As the lean, muscular black athlete stood to his feet to receive the award amid the resounding applause of the audience, tears began to flow which he could not restrain. I'll never forget his words.

> You flatter me by giving me this award, but I tell you here and now that I accept it for Brian Piccolo. Brian Piccolo is the man of courage who should receive the George S. Halas Award. I love Brian Piccolo and I'd like you to love him. Tonight, when you hit your knees, please ask God to love him too.

How often do we hear grown men say such words? "I love Brian Piccolo." What a remarkable yet rare statement! Sayers and Piccolo had cultivated more than a superficial, tough-guy relationship. Although rugged, heterosexual, competitive men to the core, authentic love had developed between these two strong athletes.

David Smith has written a timely and long-overdue book I wish men would take the time to read, *The Friendless American Male.* In it he puts his finger on a basic flaw in masculine relationships.

> Men find it hard to accept that they need the fellowship of other men. The simple request, "Let's have lunch together" is

likely to be followed with the response, "Sure, what's up?" The message is clear: the independent man doesn't need the company of another man. In fact, the image of the independent man is that he has few if any emotional needs. Therefore, men must manufacture nonemotional reasons for being together—a business deal must be discussed or a game must be played. Men often use drinking as an excuse to gather together. Rarely do men plan a meeting together simply because they have a need to enjoy each other's company.

Even when men are frequently together their social interaction begins and remains at a superficial level. Just how long can conversations about politics and sports be nourishing to the human spirit? The same male employees can have lunch together for years and years and still limit their conversation to sports, politics, and dirty jokes and comments about the sexual attractiveness of selected female workers in their office or plant. They do not know how to fellowship.[2]

Ours is a weird world in which we can't win. We men stand aloof from one another to somehow prove we are rugged individualists, yet everyone knows most of us aren't. But if we want to get close to other men, people suspect homosexuality. So we hide behind the "real man" macho mask, adhering to a counterfeit law that could easily be called "The Commandments of Masculinity":

> He shall not cry.
> He shall not display weakness.
> He shall not need affection or gentleness or warmth.
> He shall comfort but not desire comforting.
> He shall be needed but not need.
> He shall touch but not be touched.
> He shall be steel not flesh.
> He shall be inviolate in his manhood.
> He shall stand alone.[3]

Those who obey that law will never know authentic love, mark it down. Never. What the world needs now is not that phony-baloney cheap imitation, but love—authentic love.

Whom Do You Love?

Enough of others. Let's apply this to ourselves. Whom do *you* love? Of whom could *you* use the words Gayle Sayers used? "I love _____ _____?" You may feel a little cornered right now, maybe a tad defensive. "Hey, I love lots of folks . . . I don't *hate* anybody." No, I'm not talking about that. In fact, I don't believe hate is the opposite of love. Apathy is. If we treat someone with a cool indifference, if we convey to other people "I really couldn't care less," we are sending a signal loud and clear. And it doesn't say, "I love you."

So let me reword the question, "To whom are you indifferent?" You see, authentic love is in the process of building bridges, spanning chasms, reaching, risking, demonstrating, expressing, showing interest. That explains why authentic love belongs right in the middle of this book on open relationships. It is the heart-beat of a healthy body.

Watch Out for Inauthentic Traps!

Now before we get into the positive dimensions of love, let's clear away some of the negative debris. There are pitfalls to avoid in this matter of showing true love. I am indebted to Alan McGinnis once again for those three "traps" we fall into rather easily—the gusher, the pressurizer, the ramrod.[4]

The Gusher

As the name implies, the gusher is the individual who dumps tons of nice-sounding verbiage on others with a sweet, syrupy smile. You know it's mere flattery, completely lacking in depth of feeling. There is an old southern expression that describes the action of "gushers"—they are "blowing smoke on you," nothing more.

Authentic love tells the truth. Unlike gushers, those who demonstrate true love have integrity in their words. They don't indiscriminately dump the truck of artificial emotion into the ears of the public. Let's not get caught in that subtle yet popular trap.

The Pressurizer

The pressurizer is the you-scratch-my-back-since-I-scratched-yours kind of person. The reason he says "I love you" is to hear the same words said back to him. Love is not to be a lever, a manipulative grip which enables us to hold onto others. If it is authentic, it is spontaneous, devoid of hidden agendas. It is freeing not smothering. Remember Jesus' words? "You shall know the truth and the truth shall make you free."

For too many years in my marriage I confused smothering with loving. My "love" was designed to control my wife, to pressure her, to corner her. Although a "pressurizer," I really believed I was loving her.

The Ramrod

Some folks are so determined to push their love on you, they lack a sensitive spirit. They seem more bent on delivering their passionate lines and getting their script read than on finding our green-light signals that say, "I'm listening, I'm ready, I'm responsive to you."

Ramrod people are notoriously determined to travel along their one-way streets, regardless of others' reactions. Love—authentic love—remains sensitive, careful not to force its way in like a savage cutting his way through the jungle with a massive machete.

So much for what love is *not.* Let's spend the rest of this chapter on what it *is.* Instead of returning to our story in the Old Testament, let's take a break and draw our thoughts from the familiar lines of 1 Corinthians 13, the greatest treatise ever written on the subject.

An Analysis of Authentic Love

Allow me the freedom to offer a free rendering of the first three verses of 1 Corinthians 13. It's a "duke's mixture" of various paraphrases, my own translation from the original Greek, and several versions:

> If I have the ability to speak in polished and impressive fashion, or
> If I can utter sounds only angels understand, or
> If I have such a pronounced prophetic gift that I know the entire future . . . everything about everything, or
> If I possess such unswerving faith so that I can remove mountains,
> If I am so genuinely sacrificial that all my possessions are given away to the needy, or even
> If I commit the supreme act of unselfishness and go to the gas chamber for the sake of the gospel, and yet lack love, the essential ingredient; then,
> All my speaking has the sound of a hollow basin of brass and
> All my knowledge and faith is of no use and
> All my philanthropy and martyrdom gains *nothing* at all!

I find no less than four facts about true love as I meditate on these verses. And each one helps me understand just how valuable love is in having open relationships. I think you will agree.

Love Is Essential, Not Optional

First we see that love is not optional, but necessary. On no less than three occasions, Paul writes, ". . . but do not have love . . ." (vv. 1,2,3). Then he adds the clincher ". . . a noisy gong . . . nothing . . . nothing." Take away love, that essential ingredient, and it's like a car without wheels, a train without an engine, a plane without wings, a house without a foundation. Take away love and we are left with zero.

Love Is a Demonstration, Not an Inclination

When we describe love as a demonstration, it's because there is action, involvement, movement, expression. "Love is . . . love does. Love is not . . . love does not." Love doesn't sit back and snooze. It is not apathetic. It is ready and willing. It is neither passive nor indifferent. It refuses to yawn its way through life. Authentic love is demonstrative, not sterile and dull.

I distinctly remember reading about a very interesting case that came before the courts in the state of Massachusetts back in the late 1920s. It concerned a man who had been walking along a pier when suddenly he tripped over a rope and fell into the cold, deep waters of that ocean bay. He came up sputtering, screaming for help, then sank beneath the surface. For some reason he was unable to swim or stay afloat. His friends heard his faint cries in the distance, but they were too far away to rescue him. But within only a few yards was a young man lounging on a deck chair, sunbathing. Not only could the sunbather hear the drowning man plead, "Help, I can't swim," he was also an excellent swimmer.

But the tragedy is that he did nothing. He only turned his head to watch indifferently as the man finally sank and drowned.

The family of the victim was so upset by that display of extreme indifference, they sued the sunbather. The result? They lost the case. With a measure of reluctance, the court ruled that the man on the dock had no *legal* responsibility whatsoever to try to save the drowning man's life.

I suppose we could say the law agrees with Cain: "Am I my brother's keeper?" You and I have our legal right to mind our own business—to turn a deaf ear to anyone in need, to continue sunbathing while someone is drowning. We are not obligated to respond. Indifference may not be illegal, but it certainly is immoral! Which brings us back to my earlier comment: The opposite of love is apathy, not hatred. Love, sweet love, is a demonstration, not merely an inclination.

Love Is a Magnet That Draws Us Together,
Not a Wall That Keeps Us Apart

In verses 4 through 7 of 1 Corinthians 13, there are fifteen specific expressions of love, each one magnetic enough to draw people together. Just listen to them:

- Love is patient.
- Love is kind.
- Love is not jealous.
- Love does not brag and is not arrogant.
- Love does not act unbecomingly.
- Love does not seek its own.
- Love is not provoked.
- Love does not take into account a wrong suffered.
- Love does not rejoice in unrighteousness.
- Love rejoices with the truth.
- Love bears all things.
- Love believes all things.
- Love hopes all things.
- Love endures all things.
- Love never fails.

Look at that climax: "Love never fails."

When we summarize these fifteen magnetic characteristics that "never fail," I find five statements that say it all.

"I *a*ccept you as you are."
   "I *b*elieve you are valuable."
      "I *c*are when you hurt."
         "I *d*esire only what is best for you."
         "I *e*rase all offenses."

We could call that the ABCs of love. And I don't know of anybody who would turn his back on such magnetic, encouraging statements.

A number of years ago, back when the street people were

all over Southern California, we had a young man stumble into our church one Sunday evening. He was wretched looking— dirty, torn shirt, cutoffs, disheveled hair, a scraggly beard, and dazed eyes. He smelled of beer, the beach, and body odor. But one of our members saw beyond the surface and lovingly offered the stranger a seat in the meeting.

We found out later the guy had never been inside a church before in his life. He had been kicked out of his house by his parents, so he'd taken up residence in the garage, sleeping on a cot. He existed on a six pack and corn chips during the day and drugs at night. He was useless to society (but not personally worthless), and several in our congregation decided not to lose contact with him. They followed the ABCs of love and Steve could not get over it. He'd never known such attention, never felt such a magnet. He realized that these people really cared.

Slowly the walls began to crumble. Steve began to change all on his own—nothing forced. He changed from within first. His attitude changed. His habits changed. His language changed. His appearance then began to change. He even *changed his clothes!* His hunger for God and for God's Word knew no bounds. He decided to go back to work . . . then to return to school. He made things right with his folks. He and I used to talk about his relationship with others and with the Lord. Love totally won that young man! He entered seminary and ultimately graduated. He is currently ministering here in Southern Califor- nia. In fact, my older son and his wife, Curt and Debbie, now fellowship in his church. Steve is their pastor.

Love never fails . . . it draws us like a magnet.

Love Is a Long-Term Investment, Not a Quick-Return Loan

There is nothing shallow about authentic love. Nor is it a magic wand that we whip out and wave over a problem with a whoosh, hoping all the pain will go away. Real love has staying power. Authentic love is tough love. It refuses to look for ways to run away. It always opts for working through. It doesn't cop out because the sea gets stormy and rough. It's fibrous and resilient. Who knows how many of us would've walked away from our commitment many long years ago if it hadn't been for this powerful and essential ingredient deep down inside saying, "Put away that white flag. Do not quit. Don't even *tolerate* the thought." While the world around us gives the opposite counsel, love stands firm.

As an example of this, I want to close this chapter by sharing part of a letter I received. The woman who wrote it is a beautiful and rare illustration of authentic love. She and her husband renewed their marriage vows many years after they originally took them as a result of God's honoring her faithfulness.

Dear Pastor Swindoll,

. . . God has restored a marriage and rekindled a love that was virtually dead. God used your ministry, Chuck, to break, bend, and finally remold me to be more the person God wanted me to be, so I would be ready when God began His work in my husband's life.

You were doing the early part of the Romans series when I first attended Ev. Free five years ago. As I sat in the last row, I thought surely you were talking just to me, as you told of Jesus' love, forgiveness, and hope for the despairing. As my tears quietly fell, I found God's loving forgiveness and a real hope in His strength. I went home that day with my one-year-old son to a husband who worked constantly, drank heavily, and was emotionally hurting; but this time Jesus came too. You will never know the strength God gave me over the months that followed, through your insightful messages, to go on each day. Some days with peace and others by sheer endurance. How many times I wanted to run away and start over, only to walk into church and have you say, "When you are between a rock and a hard place, you stay, 'cause God's going to let you grow, if you let Him." So I stayed and let God begin His work of changing me.

I stopped praying for God to fix my marriage and change my husband, and started to consciously submit to God's will, asking Him to change me. Through the pain, He sheltered me in the shadow of His wings and I sang for joy. He brought me out of the pit of destruction and set my feet upon a rock. God was at work.

Two years ago, God removed my husband's desire for alcohol, and God did it overnight. This past summer, I decided to get off the fence, so I committed my whole life to Christ. I gave Him all those areas that I had stubbornly held on to. I said, "God, whatever it takes to bring me closer to you, you do it. I'm going to stay in this marriage and let you work your will in my life."

Well, three months later, through God's gracious timing and His circumstances, my husband accepted Jesus as his Savior. Talk about an answer to prayer! I am married to a new man, one who now loves God and wants our family to live according to God's will.

Chuck, you have said on occasion, how God can rekindle a dead love. Well, my husband and I are proof of God's caring, His power and ability to change hearts and to bring life to a dead relationship. I love my husband more now than ever before. Our priorities as a family are straight, with God first. God is so faithful, Who restored the years that the locust had eaten, Who dealt wondrously with us.

And, Chuck, our eyes fill with tears of joy when our six-year-old son says, "Thank you, Jesus, for coming into my daddy's heart and making him nice to me, and not so mean. I love my daddy."

Thank you, Pastor, for conveying God's truth and love, and being such an encouragement to me. I know God will continue to use you and the total ministry at Ev. Free to spread the truth of the gospel.

As a family, we now anticipate growing in the Lord, participating in fellowship and, as God wills, being an encouragement to others.

Sincerely,

(signed)

If authentic love can work in that woman's life, guess what. Yes, you're right. It will work for you too.

But you'll never know until you release it. You'll never know as long as it remains mere words on the pages of this book . . . or as long as it remains the lyrics to a song . . . or the lines in someone else's speech . . . or the words of some other person's letter. Yes, authentic love is the only thing there's just too little of.

DISCUSSION IDEAS AND QUESTIONS

- Of all the subjects written about in songs and poetry, love is no doubt the most popular. We've thought about it all through this chapter. What single ingredient do you most appreciate about love? Can you explain why?
- Go back over that list describing the popular idea of what men "should" be—what they "should" and "should not" do. What do you think of those things? How can a man demonstrate love without appearing weak or feminine?
- Finish the sentence, "I love ——— ———." Why are those words so hard to say?
- Discuss the "gusher," the "pressurizer," and the "ramrod." Do you have to fight falling into one of those traps? Which one?
- This may be a little painful. Is there someone you have become indifferent toward? Do you feel free to acknowledge that to others so they can pray that your attitude and response might change?
- Work your way through the four observations made about 1 Corinthians 13:1–8. Is there something special about one of them? Why?
- Review the ABCs of love. Talk about each one briefly. How about memorizing these five sentences and reviewing them the next time you meet with the group?
- Do you have children? Do they know you love them? When did you last tell them so? Do that soon. Take your time and make the conversation meaningful.

8

Needed: Shelter
for Storm Victims

CHURCHES NEED TO BE less like national shrines and more like local bars . . . less like untouchable cathedrals and more like well-used hospitals, places to bleed in rather than monuments to look at . . . places where you can take your mask off and let your hair down . . . places where you can have your wounds dressed.

It's like my Marine-buddy, recently turned Christian, said, as he lamented the absence of a place of refuge:

> . . . the only thing I miss is that old fellowship all the guys in our outfit used to have down at the slop shoot . . . we'd sit around, laugh, tell stories, drink a few beers, and really let our hair down. It was great!
>
> But now I ain't got nobody to tell my troubles to, to admit my faults to. I can't find anybody in church who will put their arms around me and tell me I'm still okay. Man, it's kinda lonely in there!

He was looking for people who demonstrated authentic love, like that discussed in chapter 7. I found myself churning, wishing it were not so. I was hoping the new Christian was nit-picking, but he wasn't. Stop and think. Where does a guy go when the bottom drops out? To whom do we Christians turn when stuff that's embarrassing or a little scandalous happens? Who cares enough to listen when we cry? Who affirms us when we feel rotten? Who will close their mouths and open their hearts? And, even though we deserve a swift kick in the pants, who will embrace us with understanding and give us time to heal without quoting verses? Without giving us a cassette tape of some sermon to listen to? Without telling a bunch of other Christians so they can "pray more intelligently"? Yeah, we need more shelters for storm victims. It's okay if they look like churches on the outside, just so folks don't act churchy on the inside. Most hurting people I meet are fed up with churchy Christians. What we *really* need is that special something many people find in the local bar. Put on your shock boots and see if you agree with the following comparison between the bar and the church.

> The neighborhood bar is possibly the best counterfeit there is to the fellowship Christ wants to give His church. It's an imitation, dispensing liquor instead of grace, escape rather than reality, but it is a permissive, accepting, and inclusive fellowship. It is unshockable. It is democratic. You can tell people secrets and they usually don't tell others or even want to. The bar flourishes not because most people are alcoholics, but because God has put into the human heart the desire to know and be known, to love and be loved, and so many seek a counterfeit at the price of a few beers.
>
> With all my heart I believe that Christ wants His church to be . . . a fellowship where people can come in and say, "I'm sunk!" "I'm beat!" "I've had it!"[1]

What if your wife is an alcoholic? Or your son recently told you he's a practicing homosexual?

Let's say your husband just walked out . . . or what if he is sexually abusing your two daughters? Or you?

Who can you turn to if you just got fired? . . . Or you just got out of jail? . . . Or your 15-year-old daughter told you last night that she was pregnant? . . . Or you beat your kids and you're scared—and ashamed? . . . Or you can't cope with your drug habit any longer? . . . Or you need professional help because you're near a breakdown?

Do you know what you need? You need a shelter. A place of refuge. A few folks who can help you, listen to you, introduce you, once again, to ". . . the Father of mercies, the God of all comfort; who comforts us in all our affliction (2 Cor. 1:3–4). Christianity may be "like a mighty army," but we often handle our troops in a weird way. We're the only outfit I've ever heard of who shoots their wounded. That's what my Marine buddy was afraid of. He had had enough of getting shot. Frankly, so have I.

SHELTERS: WHY DO WE NEED THEM?

Psalm 31 is one of those ancient hymns with an up-to-date set of lyrics. David is the composer, but he obviously got his inspiration from God. The man has run out of crutches to lean on. He's in trouble. He needs some shelter. Since there's nobody on the horizon to help, David looks up:

> In Thee, O Lord, I have taken refuge;
> Let me never be ashamed;
> In Thy righteousness deliver me.
>
> Incline Thine ear to me, rescue me quickly;
> Be Thou to me a rock of strength.
> A stronghold to save me (Ps. 31:1–2).

There it is, big as life—*refuge*. The Hebrew word is CHA-SAH, meaning "a safe place, a place of protection and secrecy." Soldiers in David's day would seek a place on the hillside that gave them a place to hide from the enemy. When they were wounded or surrounded by adverse forces or in need of security, they looked for huge boulders to hide behind, often those high up on the mountainside—a CHA-SAH hideout.

But why would David seek a place of shelter? For the same reasons *we* would! He mentions several of those reasons in Psalm 31. I find at least three: distress, sin, and adversaries.

Because We Are in Distress . . . Sorrow Accompanies Us

> Be gracious to me, O Lord, for I am in distress; My eye is wasted away from grief, my soul and my body also.
>
> For my life is spent with sorrow, And my years with sighing (Ps. 31:9–10).

Vivid, honest words—an unguarded admission. He says his eyes are red from weeping—here was a grown man who cried! He admits his life was "spent with sorrow." Things were dark, days were drab, the hope of tomorrow being different was doubtful. Joe Bayly calls such times "gray slush" days.

"A PSALM IN A HOTEL ROOM"

> I'm alone, Lord,
> alone,
> a thousand miles from home.
> There's no one here who knows my name
> except the clerk,
> and he spelled it wrong,
> no one to eat dinner with,
> laugh at my jokes,
> listen to my gripes,
> be happy with me about what happened today
> and say that's great.
> No one cares.
> There's just this lousy bed
> and slush in the street outside
> between the buildings.
> I feel sorry for myself
> and I've plenty of reason
> to.

Maybe I ought to say
I'm on top of it,
praise the Lord,
things are great;
but they're not.
Tonight
it's all
gray slush.[2]

Those are depressing, lonely times. Sorrow won't go away.
And CHA-SAH shelters are hard to come by.

Because We Are Sinful . . . Guilt Accuses Us

My strength has failed because of my iniquity, And my body
has wasted away (Ps. 31:10).

There is shame here—embarrassment. David's words drip with
guilt. He confesses that he is physically ill as a direct result of
his iniquities. It's bad enough that he feels terrible, but knowing
that much of it is his own fault, "that the vulture which feeds
on the vitals is a nestling of [his] . . . own rearing,"[3] added
insult to injury.

Who can't identify with that? Who hasn't done battle with
the slimy beast out of the swamp of guilt? Its accusations are
debilitating, and its blows are always below the belt.

In addition to distress and guilt, David mentions a third reason
for shelter—adversaries.

Because We Are Surrounded by Adversaries . . .
Misunderstanding Assaults Us

Because of all my adversaries, I have become a reproach,
Especially to my neighbors,
And an object of dread to my acquaintances;
Those who see me in the street flee from me.
I am forgotten as a dead man, out of mind,
I am like a broken vessel.
For I have heard the slander of many,

Terror is on every side;
While they took counsel together against me,
They schemed to take away my life (Ps. 31:11–13).

Did you observe how the hurting are treated?

- "I have become a reproach . . . to my neighbors."
  Ridicule
- ". . . an object of dread to my acquaintances."
  Criticism
- "Those who see me in the street flee from me . . . forgotten
  . . . like a broken vessel. . . ."
  Rejection
- "I have heard the slander of many."
  Gossip
- "They schemed to take away my life."
  Threat

We are talking misery! David was like a tiny, wounded mouse
in the paws of a huge, hungry cat. Punched, kicked, tortured
by words, and terrified with fear, the man was hanging by his
fingernails. Maybe you are, too. It's bad enough to struggle with
sorrow and live with guilt. But the final straw is the condemnation
of others—the wagging tongues and glaring eyes. And worse
yet, the silence—the absence of reassuring phone calls and hugs
of affirmation.

How we need places of relief and people of refuge! Especially
if we are committed to dropping our guard.

Refuge: How the Hebrews Handled It

Believe it or not, the Old Testament story of the Hebrews'
pilgrimage from Egypt to Canaan includes some very interesting
information about places of refuge they established. After they
had successfully invaded Canaan, the land was divided among
the Hebrews so that each tribe had territory it could call its

own. (Joshua 13–19 tells how it happened.) In their new society God did not ignore those in need, however. He instructed the leaders to set apart "cities of refuge," actual territories preserved for protection and relief.

Commanded by God

Joshua 20:1–3 speaks for itself.

> Then the Lord spoke to Joshua, saying, "Speak to the sons of Israel, saying, 'Designate the cities of refuge, of which I spoke to you through Moses, that the manslayer who kills any person unintentionally, without premeditation, may flee there, and they shall become your refuge from the avenger of blood' " (Josh. 20: 1–3).

One Old Testament scholar adds this helpful clarification:

> According to the rabbins, in order to aid the fugitive it was the business of the Sanhedrin to keep the roads leading to the cities of refuge in the best possible repair. No hills were left, every river was bridged, and the road itself was to be at least thirty-two cubits broad [about 48 feet]. At every turn were guide posts bearing the word *Refuge;* and two students of the law were appointed to accompany the fleeing man, to pacify, if possible, the avenger, should he overtake the fugitive.[4]

The point is this, every effort was made to assist, not harrass, the fugitive. People in trouble were to be protected from violent outbursts of avengers. These places of refuge were well-marked and awareness of their availability was known by all. They were not superficial tokens of concern, but well-kept and carefully maintained areas of protection.

Procedure for Entrance

The individual in trouble would run to this haven of refuge. Upon arriving, he was required to state the details of his case. He would then be admitted entrance.

And he shall flee to one of these cities and shall stand at the entrance of the gate of the city and state his case in the hearing of the elders of that city; and they shall take him into the city to them and give him a place, so that he may dwell among them (Josh. 20:4).

The New International Version captures an even more personal touch in the procedure: " . . . they are to admit him into their city and give him a place to live with them."

Please understand, those who were allowed entrance were not wanton, cold-blooded murderers. Nor were they senseless and sadistic sexual perverts and brutal rapists. They were people who had made tragic mistakes—victims of unintentional, unpremeditated offenses. Without getting carried away here by my imagination, I'd rather suspect that those who raced to these places of refuge would be under intense stress, emotionally broken by the events that had transpired, wishing in vain to erase what had happened . . . strung out, frightened, confused souls.

In recent days a Los Angeles policeman was called to a scene where someone reported trouble. He had no idea who or what was in the house in question. After asking neighbors and others several questions, he entered the dwelling with his pistol drawn. A door leading to a back bedroom was closed. He knocked. No answer. He yelled and gave his identity. Still no answer. He entered the room. Sitting on the bed was a boy with a gun pointed directly at the officer. The policeman shot first. The boy was killed. The tragedy is that the little fella was holding a toy pistol. He had been left alone that day by his mother. Words cannot describe the awful anxiety of that policeman— nor the angry reaction of the neighborhood! As I read the account and as my family and I followed the story from week to week (the officer was subsequently found to be not guilty), I thought to myself, "A classic case for a city of refuge." The man needed protection.

Can you imagine the policeman's need for reassurance? His deeply shaken father stated that he was doubtful his son would ever fully recover from the incident. Without taking away any of the grief of the dead child's mother (another need for someone to comfort and console), the sorrow, the guilt, the misunderstanding of the policeman defies description. By the way, if he were in *your* church, would there be a circle of shelter, a place for the policeman to find refuge and relief? I sincerely hope so. All too often our churches operate as though such people don't even exist. The fact is, the number of folks with this kind of need is often large.

Better than any other analogy I can think of, we are probably describing something like the old Spanish missions of yesteryear. That's perhaps as close as religious America has come to our own brand of "cities of refuge." Places of solitude, where broken people have time to recover a sense of self-worth and dignity. Where there are a few compassionate "priests" who will hear their stories and give wise counsel.

Protection from Avengers

A major purpose of those ancient places of refuge was to protect the person from those who would take it upon themselves to avenge the death of their loved one. "Now if the avenger of blood pursues him, then they shall not deliver the manslayer into his hand, because he struck his neighbor without premeditation and did not hate him beforehand" (Josh. 20:5).

For further clarification, Numbers 35 describes the difference between an intentional murder and one that was unintentional.

> But if he struck him down with an iron object, so that he died, he is a murderer; the murderer shall surely be put to death.
>
> And if he struck him down with a stone in the hand, by which he may die, and as a result he died, he is a murderer; the murderer shall surely be put to death.
>
> Or if he struck him with a wooden object in the hand, by which he may die, and as a result he died, he is a murderer; the murderer shall surely be put to death.
>
> The blood avenger himself shall put the murderer to death; he shall put him to death when he meets him.

And if he pushed him of hatred, or threw something at him lying in wait and as a result he died, or if he struck him down with his hand in enmity, and as a result he died, the one who struck him shall surely be put to death, he is a murderer; the blood avenger shall put the murderer to death when he meets him (Num. 35:16–21).

That person would not be granted asylum according to the Hebrews. But this person would:

But if he pushed him suddenly without enmity, or threw something at him without lying in wait, or with any deadly object of stone, and without seeing it dropped on him so that he died, while he was not his enemy nor seeking his injury, then the congregation shall judge between the slayer and the blood avenger according to these ordinances.

And the congregation shall deliver the manslayer from the hand of the blood avenger, and the congregation shall restore him to his city of refuge to which he fled; and he shall live in it until the death of the high priest who was anointed with the holy oil.

But if the manslayer shall at any time, go beyond the border of his city of refuge to which he may flee, and the blood avenger finds him outside the border of his city of refuge, and the blood avenger kills the manslayer, he shall not be guilty of blood because he should have remained in his city of refuge until the death of the high priest. But after the death of the high priest the manslayer shall return to the land of his possession (Num. 35:22–28).

The person was safe as long as he stayed within the boundaries of the city of refuge. But if he left . . . *zap!* Interestingly, the death of the high priest provided the manslayer with a perpetual pardon. He could then leave without fear.

Involvement of the Assembly

It is quite important that we understand what happened *within* the place of refuge. Let's return to a couple of verses:

Then the congregation shall judge between the slayer and the blood avenger according to these ordinances.

And the congregation shall deliver the manslayer from the hand of the blood avenger, and the congregation shall restore him to his city of refuge to which he fled; and he shall live in it until the death of the high priest who was anointed with the holy oil (Num. 35:24–25).

In these verses, I find three particular involvements of those who formed the assembly or "the congregation" in those ancient havens of relief. You might circle the words in your Bible for the sake of emphasis:

- "The congregation shall *judge*. . . ."
- "The congregation shall *deliver*. . . ."
- "The congregation shall *restore*. . . ."

The original term translated "judge" suggests the idea of deciding cases of controversy. It would include the necessary time and wisdom, objectivity and integrity to reflect on the evidence and to weigh the story carefully. It is the same thing asked of jurors who hear the case of the accused in courtrooms all across our country. In the days of Joshua "the congregation"—an assembly of the Levites (ancient "churchmen")—was called upon to do that.

Next, they were to *deliver* the accused from the avengers. The causative stem of the Hebrew verb translated "deliver" suggests the idea of the assembly "causing to be released," or being the cause for the removal (sometimes translated the "survival") of the accused. In other words, having heard him out and being convinced of the man's innocence, they actively pursued his recovery, his survival. There is a positive and affirming tone in the action they took.

Finally, the assembly worked together to "restore" the man fully. Again the causative stem suggests they were directly involved in the project. They not only saw to it that the man was released from guilt with full pardon, they assisted him in

his restoration of personal worth and dignity. At the death of
the high priest the man was free to return to his home.

> " 'And he shall dwell in that city until he stands before the
> congregation for judgment, until the death of the one who is
> high priest in those days. Then the manslayer shall return to his
> own city and to his own house, to the city from which he fled.' "
> So they set apart Kedesh in Galilee in the hill country of Naph-
> tali and Shechem in the hill country of Ephraim, and Kiriath-
> arba (that is, Hebron) in the hill country of Judah.
> And beyond the Jordan east of Jericho, they designate Bezer
> in the wilderness on the plain from the tribe of Reuben, and
> Ramoth in Gilead from the tribe of Gad, and Golan in Bashan
> from the tribe of Manasseh.
> These were the appointed cities for all the sons of Israel and
> for the stranger who sojourns among them, that whoever kills
> any person unintentionally may flee there, and not die by the
> hand of the avenger of blood until he stands before the congrega-
> tion (Josh. 20:6–9).

PROVIDING SHELTER TODAY: WHAT IS REQUIRED?

Those are unusual and unfamiliar names, the names of those
six cities: Kedesh, Shechem, Kirath-arba, Bezer, Ramoth, and
Golan. We've never heard of them. But we've all heard of Cincin-
nati and Dallas and Seattle and Minneapolis and Chicago and
Los Angeles. Any places of refuge there? Any assemblies in the
city where *you* live who care about the hurting enough to listen
objectively, to help folks survive, to bring people full circle back
to complete restoration? Is your town a "city of refuge"? How
about it? Waco? San Jose? Flagstaff? Portland? Fort Lauderdale?
Birmingham? Colorado Springs? Wheaton? No, let's face it,
towns are no longer designated places of refuge. Not even good,
decent towns. But within towns are some pretty important and
strategic havens of hope. They're called churches.

I'm not referring to highly polished silver sanctuaries made
mainly to be looked at. I'm talking about people—truly Christian

people, caring to the core. These folks form pockets of hope for the despairing, regardless of the appearance of the buildings where they worship.

We could call such places shelters for storm victims, hospitals for those who hurt, healing centers that specialize in wounded hearts, broken dreams, and shipwrecked souls. What is involved? What does it take to occupy those places? Listen to these words:

> We know and, to some extent realise, the love of God for us because Christ expressed it in laying down His life for us. We must in turn express our love by laying down our lives for those who are our brothers. But as for the well-to-do man who sees his brother in want but shuts his eyes—and his heart—how could anyone believe that the love of God lives in him? My children, let us love not merely in theory or in words—let us love in sincerity and in practice! (1 John 3:16–18, PHILLIPS).

If we take those words seriously, then it's quite clear what is involved:

- A willingness to go the distance for someone in trouble.
- An attitude of loving compassion for the needy.
- Availability to help in practical, tangible ways.
- Helping people feel needed and important in this high-tech, contemporary society of ours that makes us acutely aware of our insignificance.

As one clear-thinking writer put it:

> Our technological age has made us more aware of our smallness. As the world gets more and more sophisticated we increasingly feel insignificant. Our suspicion that we are not loved for who we are is confirmed daily by the impersonal nature of twentieth century living. Someone, reflecting on this observed:
>
> To the doctor I'm a patient
> To the lawyer—a client
> To the editor—a subscriber
> To the retailer—a shopper

To the educator—a student
To the manufacturer—a dealer
To the politician—a constituent
To the banker—a depositor-borrower
To the sports promoter—a fan
To the airlines—a passenger
To the minister—a parishioner
To the military—a number or a soldier

Is it any wonder that we feel dehumanized? We have come to be treated more as things than human beings. We're no longer a person but a number, no longer a human being but merely a statistic.[5]

Long enough have those who need a place of refuge occupied the local bar. It's time we made the church of Jesus Christ—the family of God—a place of refuge. It's time we held high the lamp of forgiveness, the torch of grace. Until we are willing to do that, we can forget about dropping our guards.

Several years ago I was in New York City, indeed a fascinating hub of activity. With a few hours to spare, I took the ferry out into the harbor. We circled Liberty Island (formerly Bedloe's Island), and we lingered near that famous statue, no doubt the most famous in all America.

There she stood, a proud woman, dressed in a loose robe that falls in graceful folds to the top of the pedestal on which she stands. Grasped by her left arm is a tablet bearing the date of our Declaration of Independence. Her right arm, extended high, holds a torch. At her feet is a broken shackle representing the overthrow of tyranny. One hundred tons of compassion and welcome stand as a mute testimony to the message inscribed at its base on a bronze tablet. That message is a sonnet by Emma Lazarus entitled "The New Colossus." Have you read it lately?

> Not like the brazen giant of Greek fame,
>> With conquering limbs astride from land to land;
>> Here at our sea-washed, sunset gates shall stand

A mighty woman with a torch, whose flame
Is the imprisoned lightning, and her name
   Mother of Exiles. From her beacon-hand
   Glows world-wide welcome; her mild eyes command
The air-bridged harbor that twin cities frame.
"Keep ancient lands, your storied pomp!" cries she
   With silent lips. "Give me your tired, your poor,
Your huddled masses yearning to breathe free,
   The wretched refuse of your teeming shore.
Send these, the homeless, tempest-tost to me,
   I lift my lamp beside the golden door!"

Would that inscription be appropriate on a sign in front of your church? How about your home? Or your heart? Are you engaged in the refuge business?

People needing refuge look for such statues. Tell me, where would they find one in the city or town where you live?

DISCUSSION IDEAS AND QUESTIONS

- What made the greatest impression on you in chapter 8? Why did that stand out as most important?
- Written between those lines were words like "compassion," "sympathy," "mercy," and "tolerance." Take an honest, straight-ahead look at your life. Evaluate it in light of those qualities. Where did we learn how to treat people like we do?
- David's words in Psalm 31 are to the point. Review the three reasons we need places of refuge according to this psalm. Do any of them fit you today? Explain. How about someone you know and love?
- Is there some way you (and perhaps others in your group) could reach out to your friend and convey this shelter and hope of which the chapter speaks?
- One psychologist, after watching a group of us Christians over an extended period of time, said we reminded him of a pack of porcupines on a cold winter's night. The elements push us together, but then when we get really close . . . we tend to jab and pick at one another. Have you found this to be true? Do you find yourself more comfortable around non-Christians, especially when you are struggling?
- Because there are no longer "cities of refuge," where can the hurting people in your own town turn for relief, affirmation, and recovery? Have you ever given thought to starting a ministry that reaches out to people in need . . . like alcoholics, divorcees, innocent victims of abuse, the brain-injured/retarded and their parents, the senior citizens of your community, the single parents in your church? Would you be willing to pray and take that risk?

9

Some Things Have Gotta Go!

MEANINGFUL, HEALTHY RELATIONSHIPS need the right kind of environment in which to flourish. Before we can expect to nurture open unmasked honesty, genuine assimilation, and a spirit of tolerance and compassion, *some things have gotta go!*

The same idea applies to plants and flowers. Being tender, fragile things, they need special care and the right kind of soil. Equally important is the need to protect them from enemies that assault growth. Here in Southern California we have numerous varmints that have ways of knowing every time we stick little plants in the ground. Snails, slugs, spiders, and a half dozen other ugly creatures are ready and hungry for those juicy morsels. Funny thing about them—you seldom see them. They don't carry signs that say, "Better watch out, we're dangerous!" They don't even make noise. But give them a few hours, and you can forget about a colorful garden in the spring. If you want your stuff to survive, those pests have *gotta go*. You can't simply hope they will leave. Ignoring them never works.

In God's family, in order for fragile, tender lives to survive, the enemies of growth must be exterminated. We have been saying a lot of positive things and offering affirming suggestions thus far in this book, and we've needed that emphasis. But now it's time to address some of the negatives. In order for true, first-century fellowship to flourish, we'll need to get rid of the things that attack and assault twentieth-century folks in God's family. They won't leave on their own, believe me.

Existence: Essentials for Physical Survival

On several occasions in previous pages, I have mentioned the word *body* as a synonym for the family of God, the universal church. This word picture comes from 1 Corinthians 12 where Paul develops the idea in great detail. Personally, I love word pictures. They give us mental handles with which to grasp truth. Occasionally, we can draw on the analogy to such an extent that we are able to gain fresh insight into the biblical text. This happened to me recently when I came across a paraphrase of a section in 1 Corinthians 12. The author of the paraphrase is a surgeon. And here are his words:

> The body is one unit, though it is made up of many cells, and though all its cells are many, they form one body. . . . If the white cell should say, because I am not a brain cell, I do not belong to the body, it would not for that reason cease to be part of the body. And if the muscle cell should say to the optic nerve cell, because I am not an optic nerve, I do not belong to the body, it would not for that reason cease to be part of the body. If the whole body were an optic nerve cell, where would be the ability to walk? If the whole body were an auditory nerve, where would be the sense of sight? But in fact God has arranged the cells in the body, every one of them, just as He wanted them to be. If all cells were the same, where would the body be? As it is, there are many cells, but one body.[1]

The human body consists of cells. In order for us to exist, those cells must be kept healthy. This means certain things must be present: nutrition, exercise, cleanliness, rest. And other things must be absent: disease . . . alien germs from without and wild growths from within.

No competent physician takes disease lightly. At times the doctor may suggest surgery, occasionally *radical* surgery. Usually, he will prescribe medication and occasionally a specific diet and exercise program. That's all part of the plan for a healthy existence. It's a serious (and expensive) matter.

Obedience: Key to National Preservation

Now let's shift gears from the physical body to a national body. Let's take another look at the ancient Hebrew people. Just as health is essential for our survival, *obedience* was essential for theirs.

Under Joshua, the Israelis invaded and conquered Canaan. The big war finally ended as they possessed the land God had promised them. For the first time in almost five hundred years they had their own identity. No longer were they residents on foreign soil. This was now their land. It was time to reflect and give praise to Jehovah for His faithfulness. Joshua 23 records the events that transpired.

Review of God's Faithfulness

Now it came about after many days, when the Lord had given rest to Israel from all their enemies on every side, and Joshua was old, advanced in years, that Joshua called for all Israel, for their elders and their heads and their judges and their officers, and said to them, "I am old, advanced in years.

"And you have seen all that the Lord your God has done to all these nations because of you, for the Lord your God is He who has been fighting for you.

"See, I have apportioned to you these nations which remain as an inheritance for your tribes, with all the nations which I have cut off, from the Jordan even to the Great Sea toward the setting of the sun" (Josh. 23:1–4).

God had seen them through. How good He had been to His people! He gave them rest (v. 1) after the battle ended. He had "apportioned" the land as their inheritance. What a moment! It must have brought tears to their eyes to look out across those vast spaces and realize it was now all theirs to claim. God's grace, nothing more, nothing less, nothing else!

But it was no time to stop and relax. After the brief review, Joshua announces the need to press on and do a complete job of clearing out the remaining Canaanites in the land.

Command to God's People

Lest they get the impression that it was back to "business as usual," the commander-in-chief declared:

> "And the Lord your God, He shall thrust them out from before you and drive them from before you; and you shall possess their land, just as the Lord your God promised you.
>
> "Be very firm, then, to keep and do all that is written in the book of the law of Moses, so that you may not turn aside from it to the right hand or to the left, in order that you may not associate with these nations, these which remain among you, or mention the name of their gods, or make anyone swear by them, or serve them, or bow down to them.
>
> "But you are to cling to the Lord your God, as you have done to this day.
>
> "For the Lord has driven out great and strong nations from before you; and as for you, no man has stood before you to this day.
>
> "One of your men puts to flight a thousand, for the Lord your God is He who fights for you, just as He promised you.
>
> "So take diligent heed to yourselves to love the Lord your God" (Josh. 23:5–11).

Get the picture? "Don't mess around! There's more to be done . . . some things have gotta go!" The great concern on Joshua's part is that the Hebrews might drift into a holding pattern, you know, adopt a status quo mentality.

First, he talks about their *attitude.* "Be very firm," (v. 6) he begins. He warns them about slipping to the right or to the left—about wandering from the straight path of absolute obedience to the winding paths of rationalization.

Second, he mentions their *actions.* The whole issue of concern revolved around small pockets of heathen people in Canaan, tribes people not yet driven from the territory. In today's terms, the job of "mopping up" was not complete. These Canaanites formed a threat they did not dare ignore.

Was God that serious? You decide as you read again His words of warning found in Joshua 23:7:

- Do not associate with them.
- Do not mention the names of their gods.
- Do not make anyone swear by them.
- Do not serve them.
- Do not bow down to them.

I'd call that serious, wouldn't you? That helps explain why strong words like "thrust them out" and "drive them out" (v. 5) were used by Joshua. They were to get rid of all Canaanite influence, lest they become ensnared by it.

Third, he mentions their *alternative.* They were to love the Lord their God. They were to remain distinctively His, bearing His mark, declaring His message, being uncompromisingly pure and unique.

Warning from God's Heart

If you think the warning has been serious so far, read the rest:

> "For if you ever go back and cling to the rest of these nations, these which remain among you, and intermarry with them, so that you associate with them and they with you, know with certainty that the Lord your God will not continue to drive these nations out from before you; but they shall be a snare and a

trap to you, and a whip on your sides and thorns in your eyes, until you perish from off this good land which the Lord your God has given you" (Josh. 23:12–13).

"If you ever go back. . . ." Wow! That's what I call an attention getter. Don't think of this as merely a scare tactic, a manipulative threat. This was a divine warning with consequences attached. He's saying that if they ever lose their distinctiveness by clinging to those heathens, by intermarrying with them, by identifying with them, they could count on two sure and severe consequences:

1. Jehovah would not continue as their shield of protection.
2. They would suffer unmercifully at the hands of the Canaanites.

Let's not skip over those words in verse 13 too quickly:

- "They shall become a *snare and a trap* [for your feet]."
- "They shall become *a whip* [on your sides]."
- "They shall become *thorns* [in your eyes]."

Ouch! Joshua crowds his descriptive terms together to depict the intense misery and oppression that would accompany their failure. We'll be back to those three word pictures before we're through with this chapter, so don't forget them. They are the reasons *some things have gotta go.*

Final Farewell

After delivering that sobering word of warning, the old leader says good-by.

"Now behold, today I am going the way of all the earth, and you know in all your hearts and in all your souls that not one word of all the good words which the Lord your God spoke concerning you has failed; all have been fulfilled for you, not one of them has failed.

"And it shall come about that just as all the good words which the Lord your God spoke to you have come upon you, so the Lord will bring upon you all the threats, until He has destroyed you from off this good land which the Lord your God has given you.

"When you transgress the covenant of the Lord your God, which He commanded you, and go and serve other gods, and bow down to them, then the anger of the Lord will burn against you, and you shall perish quickly from off the good land which He has given you" (Josh. 23:14–16).

Okay, what happened? Let's track the story permanently etched in the record of inspired Hebrew history. Did they do as Joshua commanded? Did they obey?

CONSEQUENCE: ACCOUNT OF PERSONAL FAILURE

We'll need to look ahead into the early part of the book of Judges, the sequel to Joshua. It traces the events that came on the heels of Joshua's death. In brief, here's what transpired:

- Judges 1:19. "They could not drive out the inhabitants of the valley . . . they had iron chariots."
- Judges 1:27. ". . . so the Canaanites persisted in living in that land."
- Judges 1:28. "And it came about when Israel became strong, that they put the Canaanites to forced labor, but they did not drive them out completely."
- Judges 1:29. The same for Ephraim, ". . . they didn't drive out the Canaanites . . . so the Canaanites *lived* . . . among them." (Can you believe it?)
- Judges 1:30. Same for Zebulun.
- Judges 1:31–32. Same for Asher . . . they "lived among the Canaanites." (Note change in wording . . . clearly, a reversal of roles.)
- Judges 1:33. Same for Naphtali, who "lived among the Canaanites."

And, now, are you ready for the ultimate?

- Judges 1:34. "Then the Amorites [a Canaanite tribe] forced the sons of Dan [a Hebrew tribe] into the hill country, for they did not allow them to come down to the valley."

The tables turned! Instead of the Hebrews' keeping the upper hand, they loosened their grip on absolute obedience, they talked themselves out of Joshua's game plan, they opted for compromise with wrong . . . and they became victims instead of victors.

Compromises like that never work. We always get burned. Even though we rationalize around our weak decisions and tell ourselves that wicked associations really won't harm us ("they'll get better, our good will rub off on their *bad!*"), we get soiled in the process.

If you put on a pair of clean white gloves on a rainy day and then go out into the backyard to the flowerbed and pick up a glob of mud, trust me, the mud will never get "glovey." The gloves will definitely get muddy. Every time. In all my forty-nine years on earth, I have never seen glovey mud. Not once. In simple terms, that's what 1 Corinthians 15:33 is saying: "Do not be deceived: 'Bad company corrupts good morals.' "

Read on:

> Then Joshua the son of Nun, the servant of the Lord, died at the age of one hundred and ten.
>
> And they buried him in the territory of his inheritance in Timnath-heres, in the hill country of Ephraim, north of Mount Gaash.
>
> And all that generation also were gathered to their fathers; and there arose another generation after them who did not know the Lord, nor yet the work which He had done for Israel.
>
> Then the Sons of Israel did evil in the sight of the Lord, and served the Baals, and they forsook the Lord, the God of their fathers, who had brought them out of the land of Egypt, and followed other gods from among the gods of the peoples who were around them, and bowed themselves down to them; thus they provoked the Lord to anger.
>
> So they forsook the Lord and served Baal and the Ashtaroth.

> And the anger of the Lord burned against Israel, and He gave them into the hands of plunderers who plundered them; and He sold them into the hands of their enemies around them, so that they could no longer stand before their enemies.
>
> Wherever they went, the hand of the Lord was against them for evil, as the Lord had spoken and as the Lord had sworn to them, so that they were severely distressed (Judg. 2:8–15).

Tragic, tragic consequences. If only they had obeyed!

Earlier I asked you to remember the snare and trap, the whip, and the thorns that are mentioned in Joshua 23:13. Here's why. If you return to the account in Judges, chapter 1, you'll find that the Hebrews endured exactly what Joshua predicted.

"Snare and trap." Not only did they allow the Canaanites to stay, they began living among them. This became "a snare and a trap" to them. By living among them, they learned their ways, they tolerated their gods, they soon adopted their lifestyle.

"Whips in your side." These are words of greater intensity. One reputable authority suggests that the Hebrew phrase could also be rendered "scourges in your side." In Judges 1:34 we find that the Amorites *forced* the Israeli Danites into the hill country, and they did not allow them to come back down and live in the valley. A classic example of being whipped in their sides by the scourge of the Amorites!

"Thorns in your eyes." Judges 3:5–6 describes how blinded the Hebrews became when they adopted the lifestyle of the heathen Canaanites and allowed themselves to be intimidated and whipped by them.

> And the sons of Israel lived among the Canaanites, the Hittites, the Amorites, the Perizzites, the Hivites, and the Jebusites; and they took their daughters for themselves as wives, and gave their own daughters to their sons, and served their gods (Judg. 3: 5–6).

That spelled inescapable consequences! The rest of the book of Judges is one account after another of compromise, weakness, tyranny, and defeat.

Resistance: Hope for Open Relationships

If you've stayed with me thus far, you're to be commended! Ancient history is sometimes tough sledding, but when it is biblical history, it is rewarding, as you'll see. The application of all this to our study on open relationships will prove helpful, I believe.

Let me review where we've been. Just as the human body cannot grow and survive unless disease is removed . . . and just as the national body of Israel could not remain strong and healthy unless Canaanite lifestyle was removed, so it is in the body of Christ. If our resistance breaks down, alien germs will cause us to lose our health and hinder our ability to function.

Things That Become Snares and Traps Have Gotta Go!

It is often the subtle things that become snares and traps for us—usually unspoken things that we communicate in our body language and our looks . . . attitudes that speak volumes to young, tender, and fragile folks struggling to survive.

Let me list a few such snares and traps:

Judgmental spirit	Unkind, unfriendly remarks
Intolerance	Sophistication
Suspicion	Cynicism
Prejudice	Unforgiving reaction
Pride	Condemning looks
Exclusive attitude	Unapproachability

We may not tell too many people off, but it sure is easy for us to freeze them out! And I do not believe we can expect to encourage and nourish open, unguarded relationships in an atmosphere of snares and traps, so some things have gotta go. What better place to start ridding ourselves of these snares and traps than the list just mentioned!

Things That Become Whips Have Gotta Go!

People come to us personally, or they visit our churches, greatly in need of affirmation, authentic love, compassion, big doses of esteem, hope, and forgiveness—all those things you've been reading about in the first eight chapters. They need release from the strangle hold of self-imposed guilt and relief from the I'm-no-good-I'm-only-a-worm syndrome.

They may reach out in one of many ways . . . but if "the whip" routine is there to assault, the results are often disastrous. Here are a few whips which you may have either encountered or used yourself!

- Attempting to pressure people to "straighten up" or "snap out of it" before they're able to get on their feet.
- Forcing people to become more and more like we are— "if you really want to be mature."
- Expecting adherence to highly structured demands, tight-fisted rules, and rigid requirements.
- Placing the painful twist of legalistic demands, that is, tightening the screws on others to give up certain habits and adapt to our set of preferences or convictions, the old "shape up or ship out" stiff-arm.

Whips like these will beat you to death, like scourges in your side. And you'll not be given the freedom to learn, to discover, to fail, or to be your own person.

Things That Become Thorns Have Gotta Go!

"Thorns" are from without. They are things we bring to the body that cause offense and disease to other members—alien germs that enter into weakened, bruised, and broken places. And remember, thorns blind.

Now let's take a look at a few such thorns:

- Persisting in unchecked, willful sin without genuine repentance.
- Deliberately operating under the control of the flesh, walking contrary to the will of God in unashamed carnality.
- Hiding behind blame or self-pity or some other rationalization to justify wrong actions . . . and refusing to face the truth.
- Living a lie, taking unfair advantage of young, tender believers who are impressionable and naive.
- Practicing hypocritical spiritual leadership, ignoring the fact that some day the truth will be known and many will be disillusioned.

Enough said. These things have gotta go!

I close on a positive note with these wise words—not my own—that describe the inestimable value of affirmation. I wish there were some way you and I could be sufficiently convinced to commit them to memory.

> Life breaks down not so much because of the terrible things that happen to us. Life breaks down because so few good things have happened to us. Just a few along the way can be like branches we can cling to as we climb up a mountain trail. No matter how steep the ascent, we can make it, if from time to time along the trail someone communicates to us that he or she loves us and therefore we are important.[2]

DISCUSSION IDEAS AND QUESTIONS

- Go back to the first part of chapter 9 and reread the surgeon's paraphrase of those verses out of 1 Corinthians 12. Talk about how it applies to the body of Christ. In what condition are the "cells" you spend your time with—the other Christians in your life? Are they strengthening your walk?

- As we looked through Joshua 23, we found some strong words against compromise and associating too closely with the wrong crowd. What have you found that helps you maintain good and healthy associations? If this is a battle, talk about your struggle. Ask for prayer.

- Remember the snares and traps, whips, and thorns? It might be helpful to go back into the chapter and refresh your memory. In your own words, define each of the three.

- As you think about your home, are there any snares and traps, whips, or thorns that need to be removed? It may take an exceptional amount of courage, but try to name a few.

- On a positive note, can you think of a Christian who might be in need of some affirmation? Maybe there is someone who has suffered from the attack of another's tongue or attitude. How about giving him or her a phone call . . . or writing a brief letter of sincere interest? Make yourself available as a healing agent. It could be exciting!

10

Choose
for Yourself

IT IS EASY TO GET so hot and bothered about the insignificant, we miss the significant . . . to focus on little petty stuff with such intensity, we lose sight of the big picture.

I was reminded of that when I read of the crash of an Eastern Airlines jumbo jet in the Florida Everglades. The plane was the now-famous flight 401, bound for Miami from New York City, with a heavy load of holiday passengers. As the huge aircraft approached the Miami Airport for its landing, a light that indicates proper deployment of the landing gear failed to come on. The plane flew in a large, looping circle over the swamps of the Everglades while the cockpit crew checked out the light failure. Their question was this: Had the landing gear actually not deployed or was it just the light bulb that was defective?

To begin with, the flight engineer fiddled with the bulb. He tried to remove it, but it wouldn't budge. Another member of the crew became curious and tried to help him out . . . and then another. By and by, if you can believe it, all eyes were on the little light bulb that refused to be dislodged from its socket. No one noticed that the plane was losing altitude. Finally, it flew right into the swamp. Many were killed in that plane crash. While an experienced crew of high-priced and seasoned pilots messed around with a seventy-five-cent light bulb, an entire airplane and many of its passengers were lost. The crew momentarily forgot the most basic of all rules in the air—"Don't forget to fly the airplane."

That same thing can happen in a local church. The pastor can be so busy fighting petty fires and focusing so much of his attention on insignificant issues that he loses sight of what church is all about. It is possible for the church to have so many activities, programs, clubs, projects, committee meetings, banquets, and community involvements—so many wheels spinning without really accomplishing anything of eternal significance—that the congregation forgets its primary objective. Many churches are like that impressive invention which had hundreds of wheels, coils, gears, pulleys, belts, bells, and lights which all went around and rang and flashed at the touch of a button. When the inventor was asked about the function of the weird machine, he replied, "What does it do? Oh, it doesn't *do* anything, but doesn't it run beautifully?"

A PRIMARY OBJECTIVE

Ask around. See if folks in your church know why the ministry exists. Be ready for a surprise. Don't be shocked if most of them shrug and say, "Oh, I don't know—to hear somebody preach, I guess . . . we're here just to be fed." It is not an exaggeration to say that the common opinion in many evangelical churches is just that—"We're here to be informed." As important as preaching may be (and I really believe in good preaching), it is only a part of the greater objective. The church is called a body, remember? We gather for more reasons than simply to take in more and more food.

Think of your family. I doubt that you would say, "Our family is a family because we eat together. That's why we are in existence. We eat often and we eat a lot. The food is so nourishing, so well-prepared, and always served right on time. We love to eat! Because of that, we're a family." No, a family shows itself to be a family in ways other than gathering at a dining-room table loaded with food. For instance:

- By how it responds to those who hurt.
- By the way it listens when family members talk.
- By the extent to which it reaches out and supports those who cannot keep up.
- By how it communicates affirmation . . . how it sticks together through the hard times . . . how it laughs at fun times.
- By the basis on which it establishes accountability, responsibility, and evaluation.
- By allowing room for its members to express true feelings— joy, grief, anger, elation, doubt, disagreement, anticipation, loss, disillusionment, disappointment, pleasure, pain—the full spectrum.

It is easy to see that a family is much more than taking in good food. And so is a church. The church is a training base, and we must never forget it! It is a place where God's family members are encouraged to grow; to learn; to exercise; to find rest, refreshment, and stability for facing life's realities . . . a body of fellow strugglers who meet together and relate openly, honestly, and freely. It is a place of prayer and quiet solitude . . . an anvil where ideas are hammered out and convictions take shape . . . a hospital for those needing time and room to heal . . . a place where compassion and forgiveness and grace are dispensed just as readily and regularly as information. That's the big picture. If we lose sight of that we're headed for a swamp, full throttle.

Let me go back to the example of the Statue of Liberty I used previously, to those moving words of Emma Lazarus: "Give me your tired, your poor, your huddled masses . . . the

wretched . . . the homeless, tempest-tost."[1] I honestly wonder
if today's church hasn't rewritten those lines to read:

> "Give me your ignorant, and I will instruct
> (but don't expect us to get involved)."

Or:

> "Give me your wealthy, and I will buy and invest
> (but don't ask us to relate)."

Or:

> "Give me your strong and your willing, and I will keep
> them busy
> (but don't expect much compassion)."

In other words, "If you have life pretty much together; if your
theology is screwed down tightly; if you're willing to give, but
not in need of receiving anything other than some sermons,
songs, and superficial talk, let's get together." Somehow, that
doesn't seem anywhere near the message Jesus modeled. He
touched people, He made room for relationships. He taught,
but He never taught just for the sake of filling up heads like
gas tanks at a pump. With Him love was linked with truth;
compassion was never far behind command. The balance in His
life makes a bold statement, doesn't it?

If you pick up nothing else from these pages, don't miss this:
Unguarded, open relationships within the body of Christ are
just as important as the nourishing, accurate dispensing of scriptural truth. We need both. There must be meaningful fellowship,
not just scholarship. To have one without the other results in
an unbalanced and unhealthy church. It really is a matter of
choice, however. No one can force a congregation to believe
this.

DECISIONS THAT ENCOURAGE RELATIONSHIPS

Let's return to the biblical story we've been following throughout this book. We have come through the Exodus and the sea
with Moses and the Hebrews. We have arrived at Canaan,

invaded and inhabited the country, and heard the warnings about snares and traps, whips, and thorns. We have come to admire Joshua as a courageous leader who told the truth, regardless. The sad news is that he is near death. He knows it. As he looks into the faces of those he's led into the promised land, he has mixed emotions. He is pleased at what they have accomplished, but he is uneasy over their tendency toward passivity. Like a wise parent with an irresponsible child, Joshua knows there are painful consequences awaiting the people if they do not heed God's warnings. He decides to tell it straight. They need to hear it before he passes off the scene.

The Major Factor

Who knows how many times he must have repeated his concern? "Don't forget to finish the task. Those Canaanites must be removed. Keep on loving and obeying Jehovah. Don't lose your distinctiveness now that you are living in homes you didn't build and eating from trees you didn't plant. Stay strong!" Familiar words are these:

> " 'And you crossed the Jordan and came to Jericho; and the citizens of Jericho fought against you, and the Amorite and the Perizzite and the Canaanite and the Hittite and the Girgashite, the Hivite and the Jebusite. Thus I gave them into your hand.
>
> " 'Then I sent the hornet before you and it drove out the two kings of the Amorites from before you, but not by your sword or your bow.
>
> " 'And I gave you a land on which you had not labored, and cities which you had not built, and you have lived in them; you are eating of vineyards, and olive groves which you did not plant' " (Josh. 24:11–13).

God had done it all. But there is one major factor He left for them to act upon . . . one thing that could make or break their entire future. Do you know what it was? They had the freedom to choose for themselves. Joshua says so.

"Now, therefore, fear the Lord and serve Him in sincerity and truth; and put away the gods which your fathers served beyond the River and in Egypt, and serve the Lord.

"And if it is disagreeable in your sight to serve the Lord, choose for yourselves today whom you will serve: whether the gods which your fathers served which were beyond the River, or the gods of the Amorites in whose land you are living; but as for me and my house, we will serve the Lord" (Josh. 24:14–15).

Personal righteousness does not happen because somebody requires and commands it of us. Obedience cannot be legislated. Godliness cannot be forced. People don't live pure lives due to warnings and threats. These things must come from the heart as a result of right choices.

Are you a superintense brother or sister—the type who relies on firm, strong commands and a good deal of push and shove? Let me level with you. I'll drop my guard and admit that I spent far too many years in my life marching to that drumbeat . . . lots of frowns and demands, long drawn-out requirements that prompted guilt but never did much for desire. People got the message, but they really didn't change that much. I burned up enormous amounts of internal energy, but in the final analysis most of it was for naught. That method is about as effective as pushing a rope.

People respond much better to personal models than to verbal demands. They are motivated much more by the Joshua method of leadership ("as for me and my house, we will serve the Lord, but you must choose for yourself") than by the rip-snorting, smoke-and-fire screams and threats of the uptight types. It's been my observation in recent years (I learned this so late!) that most Christians really don't want to live mediocre lives, but neither do they desire to be driven like cattle. Folks respond more like sheep than steers.

I received this letter recently.

Dear Chuck,

I was deeply moved by your talk on Martin Luther. In fact, I tried to sing with you at the end, but I cried instead. I feel so small. Our heros look so big, so deep, so much better than me. I'm so comfortable. And so mediocre.

I want to know something. When you were 27, were you like you are now? Had you already read all the right books? Did you know all the hymns? More importantly, were you as deep as you are now? Was Christ so real in your life that your words pierced people's hearts? I ask that because I want to know if there is any hope for me. I am not broad, nor very deep. I wasn't raised in the church. I don't know the hymns. I still have to read them in the hymnal. I wasn't raised to be a big reader, either. I want to read the right books, but I get very frustrated when I go to the Christian bookstore. Who needs books like "Pray Your Way to Big Bucks," "If You're Sick—You're a Lousy Christian," "Positive Thinking—Never Say 'Sin' " or a book full of goofy rhymes to replace talking with God.

I've also heard you say that one becomes like those with whom he spends his time. I'm surrounded by mediocre people. The more I mature in the Lord, the fewer people I find worth imitating. I'm not so mature, though, that God is the only model . . . you are a model for me. . . . I want to know—are you like my other "models"? Do you rip your wife apart in front of other married people? . . . Do you talk big but turn wimpy when it's time for action? Are you worth imitating?

How can I be excellent? I don't care about impressing anyone. I just don't want to be mediocre.

Do you know what that young man wants? He wants a model. He wants to be sure, however, that the model is authentic. I appreciate his questions. He's looking for ways to move from mediocrity to maturity, but he is not anxious to jump on any bandwagon. He's struggling with some basic choices. He doesn't need a preacher like me screaming at him to shape up or ship out. He needs room to work through some choices so that his life reflects genuine godlikeness. The major factor is this: *He must choose for himself.* No one else can make him godly.

So it was in Joshua's day. The leader had made up his mind. He and his household would serve the Lord, no question about that. But when it came to everyone else, "Choose for yourselves today whom you will serve. . . ." My! I wish I had adopted that method of leading earlier in my ministry. I could have saved myself so much anxiety, and the sheep I led would have been encouraged by my model rather than harrassed by my demands.

Three Essential Parts

With the freedom to choose, the Hebrews declared their intentions. Drawn by Joshua's commitment, they chose to align themselves with his cause. His desires became their desires *by choice*. His dedication became their dedication *by choice*. If you look deeply into this section of the narrative you can find three essential parts in their decision.

1. They chose to "fear the Lord" (v. 14). In other words, they chose to hold Him, not the Canaanite culture, in awesome respect, to revere Him, to let Him be the standard of their lives.

2. They chose to "serve the Lord" (v. 14). It was their voluntary decision to "serve Him in sincerity." On three subsequent occasions they declared their unequivocal commitment to follow Him—"we will serve the Lord" (vv. 18,21,24).

3. They chose to "obey His voice" (v. 24). They decided to listen to His counsel and to heed His advice. They deliberately announced their decision to respond in obedience.

Joshua must have beamed from ear to ear. He responded with these words: "You are witnesses against yourselves that you have chosen for yourselves the Lord, to serve Him." And they said, "We are witnesses" (Josh. 24:22).

There it is again, "you have chosen for yourselves." There isn't anything more encouraging to the leader of a congregation than this, when they voluntarily decide to obey the Lord, regardless. Why? Because choices have a direct bearing on behavior.

> . . . we have very little direct control over our emotions, but we have maximum control over our behavior. In other words, we can change our feelings with our will only to a certain degree, whereas our behavior is under the complete and maximum control of our will.[2]

This helps pastors realize that messages which simply arouse a lot of emotion aren't nearly as vital as those directed to the will. Emotions heat up or cool off within a brief span of time, but when truth makes an impact on the will, lives begin to change.

Ultimate Benefit

What ultimately happens when our choices are linked to God's directives? (This is the best part of all!) He offers His true and lasting support. He takes us at our word, and He weaves His power into the fabric of our lives. In place of our turmoil, He brings peace. Instead of our weakness and instability, He provides strength and stability.

Are you beginning to get serious about dropping your guard? Have you come to the place where you're willing to admit that a church is more than a pulpit and pews? Do relationships matter enough to you that it's worth the effort and risk for you to get involved in others' lives? Are those some of the choices you are making? If so, I have some great news for you. God will honor and support such choices. He will supplement your desires with His ability. Even when you don't realize it, He will be working behind the scenes, bringing many of your dreams to reality.

When we act upon scriptural truth, the Lord offers His divine assistance. The secret, however, is that we make the right choices . . . not just consider the options.

One of the most familiar stories Jesus told is recorded in Matthew 7:24–27. As soon as you begin reading it, you'll remember it.

> "Therefore every one who hears these words of Mine, and acts upon them, may be compared to a wise man, who built his house upon the rock.
> "And the rain descended, and the floods came, and the winds blew, and burst against that house; and yet it did not fall, for it had been founded upon the rock.

"And every one who hears these words of Mine, and does not act upon them, will be like a foolish man, who built his house upon the sand.

"And the rain descended, and the floods came, and the winds blew, and burst against that house; and it fell and great was its fall" (Matt. 7:24–27).

What an amazing difference! A close look will reveal the reason one house stood and the other house fell. The first was occupied by "one who hears these words of Mine and acts upon them," but the second was occupied by "one who hears . . . and does not act upon them." It boiled down to choice, didn't it? Jesus isn't concerned with literal houses and literal rocks and sand. These are symbols of life and the choices we make that result in whether we stand or fall. If right choices are made, it's like building our lives on rock. They will stand the test of time.

Bottom Line: What Do You Choose?

Maybe it's time to ask a couple of hard questions. Are you one who hears and then acts on what God says? Or are you one who simply hears and keeps all the options open? It sure is easy to mess around with insignificant stuff and miss the big picture. Remember flight 401? You and I are surrounded by people who focus on needless incidentals and wind up in the swamp.

Jesus helps clear away the smoke screen. He's a master at bringing us to terms with things that really matter. He not only offers us His insight so we can see the big picture, He offers us Himself. Perhaps you have been so busy doing church work, keeping all those wheels and gears turning, you've missed the most basic point of all . . . we cannot be rightly related to others until we are rightly related to Him. Coming to know Him, by faith, moves our lives from shifting sand to a solid rock. Could it be—could it *possibly* be—that you have lived all your life having never made the most important choice of all? Not one of us is programmed to be righteous. It's a matter of choice. Choosing to let Christ come into your life is not insignificant. He is the only One who can give you the wisdom you need to handle the rains, the floods, and the winds that are sure to assault your life. Give some serious thought to turning your life over to Christ. Believe me, it's no insignificant decision.

In fact, in comparison to choosing Christ, all other decisions fall into the category of seventy-five-cent light bulbs.

DISCUSSION IDEAS AND QUESTIONS

- This has been a chapter about the value of right choices. Time and again we've considered how important they are. Why is that true? Can you think of a particular decision you made that had life-changing ramifications? Talk about it.
- In thinking about the basic purpose of the church, answer this question in your own words: What's the reason for the existence of the body of Christ? Try to be brief and to the point.
- Is your day full of what seems to be seventy-five-cent-light-bulb concerns instead of big-picture essentials? Discuss the frustrations that accompany such struggles.
- Joshua's style of leadership is admirable. He modeled the message he proclaimed. He didn't demand or force the people to adopt his convictions, but he did declare where he stood. Do you find that appealing? Are you more persuaded to follow Joshua's approach or do you prefer a stronger stance? If you are a leader, what is your style?
- As the people voluntarily aligned themselves with Joshua and his household, they chose to fear, to serve, and to obey the Lord. What did that imply? When would it be most difficult to carry out?
- Read again the story Jesus told (Matt. 7:24–27). Talk a little about building a life on sand. What does "sand" represent? Can a life built on sand ever be shifted over to a rock foundation? How? Be very specific.
- Go back to the last page of chapter 10. Read the section under "Bottom Line." Have you ever made that choice? Describe in a few sentences how and when you chose to have Christ come into your life.

11

The Necessity
of Accountability

I DRIVE A SPOTLESS, white 1979 Volkswagen Superbeetle converti-
ble. It's a fun little car, and I treat it with the kind of kid-
glove care and massive doses of T.L.C. that only vintage car
lovers can understand. Hopefully, it will be around for many,
many years. There are few things to compare with the feeling
of zipping along with the top down on a breezy sun-drenched
afternoon. It sorta flushes out my nervous system and keeps
me from getting too serious about myself. There's only one problem, I'm a marked man! My white and shining little bug (with
Porsche wheels and Michelin sneakers!) has a way of attracting
a lot of attention, even when I'm not aware of it, which is illustrated by the following letter that I received several months ago.

Dear Pastor Chuck:

Hello! Just a short note to say that we have been enjoying
very much your series on relationships. Your message last Sunday
on "Choose for Yourself" was especially inspiring as we were

motivated to make a definite conscious decision to follow and trust Jesus Christ.

A group of men from our Sunday school class meets each Wednesday morning at seven in Fullerton to discuss and pray over some of the many choices involved in being husbands, friends, employees, etc., from a Christian point of view. As a matter of fact, just today we saw someone make a definite, conscious decision as two of us drove from La Habra to Fullerton for our weekly time together. I'll set the scene. . . .

After setting our alarms at what we thought was plenty early to allow time to shower, shave, and take out the trash before leaving, we found ourselves late! Well, after meeting at my friend's house to share a ride, we headed down Harbor Boulevard towards Fullerton, late and probably going a little too fast! Yep, you guessed it, good ol' Murphy caught us. You know, he's the guy that said, "If a traffic light can change when you're late, IT WILL!" So, there we sat, 7:10 A.M. at the intersection of Harbor and Brea Boulevard, late for our 7 A.M. meeting and thinking we'd have to wait through the whole cycle of light changes.

Using the time to tuck in our shirts and comb our hair, we suddenly noticed a small, white, soft-shelled insect of a car headed up Brea Boulevard from west of Harbor, also caught in the same exact predicament—STUCK AT THE LIGHT! The surprisingly familiar face inside looked rushed, yet willing to wait it out. All of a sudden, the driver's head (almost as if powered by an outside force) furtively and daringly glanced right, then left, into the rear-view mirror, and WHOOOOSH!!!! Right through the red light!

"Brother, was that who I thought it was running that red light?"

"If you thought it was who I thought it was, then who you thought it was was *exactly* who I thought it was!"

"What shall we do?"

"Let's write up a complete account of this late breaking story and submit it to *Moody Monthly, Christianity Today, Leadership, Wittenburg Door,* and *Dad's Only* ("Come on, Junior, it's Saturday morning, so let's go run some red lights together!").

Before mailing off our own "Choose for Yourself" sermon, we were struck from above with an option that, if exercised, would alleviate the whole scene of the TV crews on the front porch, crying wife, and "talk to my lawyer" episodes. It just so happens that the same two of us who observed the crime have breakfast together every Wednesday at 8 A.M. after our small-group at

> Randy's Coffee Shop in Fullerton. We felt if that certain individual who drives the white, soft-shelled insect would show up for breakfast on either Wednesday, November 25, or on Wednesday, December 2, at 8 A.M. at Randy's Coffee Shop, we could avoid the whole media smear! The article would be mailed at 9:00 A.M. on Wednesday, December 2, if there's a no-show. If you do show, we'll identify ourselves and even treat you to breakfast . . . if we choose . . . CHOOSE FOR YOURSELF!!!!

Naturally, it was *unsigned*. Well, I was caught redhanded by the rascals. So I decided to show up at the coffee shop bright and early on November 25. I stuck a big sign on my shirt that read "Guilty as Charged." I walked up to the startled waitress at 7:45 that morning and asked her to seat me at a table where several could join me. I told her I was meeting with some Pharisees that morning. She put some menus down and walked away shaking her head. At eight o'clock sharp in they walked! When we all had a laugh at my sign, I turned it over. On the back I had written "He who is without sin, let him cast the first stone!" They bought my breakfast.

If I live to the ripe old age of 100, I doubt that I'll ever forget that whole episode. Every time I'm tempted to run a light, the letter comes back to haunt me . . . one of the many benefits of accountability!

Accountability: What It Is and Isn't

I've purposely saved the subject of accountability for the latter part of my book. The major reason for this is that I wanted you to understand the full picture of unguarded, close, loving, meaningful relationships *before* we dealt with this particular subject. Without that backdrop, accountability could carry with it a harsh and abrasive sound.

Just the term sounds pretty legal, doesn't it? And rightly so, for that's the way we use it most often. If we go to the bank and secure a loan, we are legally responsible to pay it back.

That's *financial* accountability. If we get a job, we agree to work under certain terms and regulations. That's *occupational* accountability. If we enroll in a university and decide on a curriculum that requires our being a student at the school, studying under various faculty members, we must fulfill the course requirements, including homework and examinations in order to get a degree. That's *academic* accountability.

There's usually no problem with this kind of accountability—we consider it a matter of good business dealings or standard educational expectations. But when someone mentions our being accountable to others outside those "legal" settings, our tendency is to recoil. We resist the idea of mixing something as exacting as accountability with something as loving and encouraging as our spiritual lives, don't we? To be accountable to a boss is not only acceptable, it's essential. In fact, those who resist it and don't cooperate with it wind up unemployed. But why not be accountable to someone who loves me and wants what is best for me? What's so wrong with *friendship* accountability, especially if it has what it takes to improve and enhance our walk with God? Perhaps our secret resistance is yet another proof of what isolationists we really are.

Nontechnical Definition

Rather than scope out some scholarly definition, let's consider this practical one. When I use the term *accountability*, I have several things in mind as it relates to the subject matter of this book. Being accountable includes:

- Being willing to explain one's actions.
- Being open, unguarded, and nondefensive about one's motives.
- Answering for one's life.
- Supplying the reasons why.

Again, if you take away the context of love and affirmation, those aspects of accountability could seem terribly galling. And if we erased the all-important factor of friendship, we could find ourselves saying, "That's none of your business." So let's not do that. Let's understand that when I speak of accountability, I'm referring to one of the involvements, a by-product if you please, of a deep and meaningful relationship with one or a few intimate friends. In that sense, therefore, I'm talking about voluntary accountability.

The more I think about accountability, the more I realize why it is so rare. It requires at least four character traits that are not normally found in folks who are satisfied to live mediocre lives—and that's a whole lot of people! The qualities are:

- *Vulnerability* . . . capable of being wounded, open, and unguarded. Nondefensive.
- *Teachability* . . . anxious to learn. Humble, quick to hear, willing to change, inviting advice.
- *Honesty* . . . committed to the truth. Hating anything phony, counterfeit, or false. Models sincerity.
- *Availability* . . . touchable, accessible. Can be interrupted. Willing to meet on a regular basis.

See why this is so rare? Offhand, how many people can you name who possess such valuable traits?

Accountability on a personal level is not that unusual. Or perhaps I should say *should* not be that unusual. When two people marry and choose to give up their independent single life, they opt for mutual accountability. In most marriages I'm acquainted with (this certainly applies to mine), when one of the mates is gone much, much longer than the other anticipated, an explanation is expected and willingly provided. If one goes home and finds a sleek new speedboat in the driveway, more is expected than an exuberant, "Isn't it beautiful!"

Pertinent Scripture

What is true between partners in a marriage is equally true among members in the body of Christ. Take a look at Hebrews 13:16–17:

And do not neglect doing good and sharing; for with such sacrifices God is pleased.

Obey your leaders, and submit to them; for they keep watch over your souls, as those who will give an account. Let them do this with joy and not with grief, for this would be unprofitable for you (Heb. 13:16–17).

I'd say that's pretty clear, wouldn't you? Pastors, priests, bishops, and other leaders whom God selects for places of great responsibility (even though they themselves are imperfect and human) are those who "keep watch over your souls." And what about the leaders? Are they not also responsible? Indeed they are! They, too, need people around them who have the freedom to ask why and who feel the liberty to talk about any issue.

Solomon offers good counsel: "Faithful are the wounds of a friend, But deceitful are the kisses of an enemy" (Prov. 27:6). We'll come back to this verse later on in the chapter, but let's probe below the surface of the words for a few moments. Some time ago I did a careful investigation of this proverb, searching out the original meanings of the terms and some of the syntactical significance of the Hebrew language. I came up with a paraphrase:

Trustworthy are the bruises caused by the wounding of one who loves you, but deceitful are the kisses (of flattery) from those who hate you.

When someone knows us well enough and therefore loves us deeply enough to "wound" us with the truth, the bruises that remain (and they *are* bruises) are trustworthy, reliable. This is true for both the leader and the led. Please note that everybody is not "fair game." Some people who believe they have "the gift of criticism" (every church has a few) think they have the right to take on whomever. But this proverb says that reproofs from *"a friend"* (one who knows you well and loves you intensely) are reliable and beneficial. Strangers or casual acquaintances do not have the wholesale freedom to punch people's lights out. That isn't accountability, that's brutality. Solomon is not advocating a watchdog mentality among casual acquaintances. He's attempting to convince us of the value of having a few folks so near and dear to us that they have the freedom to "bruise" us with the truth. Such friends are worthy of our trust.

Extreme Dangers

It's at this very juncture that some things need to be added, lest I turn a few who read these words into a pack of vultures with a Gestapo mindset. Actually, there are two extremes we need to be aware of and guard against—being too severe and being too loose.

1. *We are not to be too severe.* When I think of this extreme, I think of a man who lived toward the end of the first century. His name was Diotrephes. John mentions him in his third letter:

> I wrote something to the church; but Diotrephes, who loves to be first among them, does not accept what we say.
>
> For this reason, if I come, I will call attention to his deeds which he does, unjustly accusing us with wicked words; and not satisfied with this, neither does he himself receive the brethren, and he forbids those who desire to do so, and puts them out of the church.
>
> Beloved, do not imitate what is evil, but what is good. The one who does good is of God; the one who does evil has not seen God (3 John 9–11).

What a savage! I get the distinct impression that Diotrephes would have made a great first-century Hitler . . . or Attila the Hun. I mean, when that guy took over the leadership, he *took over.* John correctly condemns such oppressive measures.

The whole tenor of Scripture stands against such a legalistic, militant, rigid accountability. It is pharisaical and judgmental, sadly lacking in servanthood. This extreme style uses accountability to control and manipulate people, actions never justified in Scripture.

2. *We are not to be too loose.* The Corinthians fell into this trap. They were the classic "live and let live" congregation who

had no standard of purity and weren't about to concern themselves with such.

> It is actually reported that there is immorality among you, and immorality of such a kind as does not exist even among the Gentiles, that someone has his father's wife.
>
> And you have become arrogant, and have not mourned instead, in order that the one who had done this deed might be removed from your midst.
>
> For I, on my part, though absent in body but present in spirit, have already judged him who has so committed this, as though I were present (1 Cor. 5:1–3).

These folks sound a lot like the Hebrews in the book of Judges where everyone wound up doing what was right in his own eyes. But the sad fact is that in Corinth they not only refused to hold the man accountable and deal with his sinful, shameful, scandalous actions, they justified their actions by claiming *grace* as their reason.

Both extremes are dangerous and damaging. I am not advocating that we become severe and stern saints with a watchdog mentality like Diotrephes. But neither is the answer a casual, "who-really-cares?" approach like the Corinthians employed. Obviously, the world prefers the latter extreme, and this has its own tragic consequences. Not only does secular society "live and let live," it also advocates "die and let die."

I was reminded of that when I read the report of the late actor William Holden's death. It began:

> William Holden was a private man, and he died a very private death. Alone in his apartment in Santa Monica, Calif., he bled to death from a gash in his forehead caused by a drunken fall against his bedside table. It was four or five days later that his body was found. He was 63.[1]

Does that seem as incredible to you as it does to me? There was a famous man over 60 years old whose name was a household word in the film industry and among moviegoers the world over.

He'd been making movies for over four decades, yet he was dead for "four or five days" before he was found . . . or even missed. How could it be? There's a hint in the closing paragraph of that same article: "Holden guarded his privacy with increasing vigilance."

Privacy is one thing. We all need it, no one would deny that. But being so out of touch and unaccountable? That's the part no one can justify. There are times when it is essential that someone say *something*. Sometimes it's a matter of life and death that somebody speak up.

Take the case of Martin Niemoller, a Lutheran pastor in Germany in the 1930s. Here is his often-quoted, honest confession:

> In Germany they came first for the communists, and I didn't speak up because I wasn't a communist. Then they came for the Jews, and I didn't speak up because I wasn't a Jew. Then they came for the trade unionists, and I didn't speak up because I wasn't a trade unionist. Then they came for the Catholics, and I didn't speak up because I was a Protestant. Then they came for me, and by that time no one was left to speak up.

Examples from Scripture

There is nothing quite so reassuring as scriptural support. Experience is fine and illustrations from life help bring light on the subject, but when we can find passages and verses from the Bible, we've got an open-and-shut case. Is accountability scriptural? Does God really stand behind the things we are considering in this chapter? Indeed he does.

Vertical and Horizontal Accountability

It is clearly stated in the New Testament that the members of Christ's body are accountable to the Head. Who hasn't thought of the implications of Jesus' words?

"The good man out of his good treasure brings forth what is good; and the evil man out of his evil treasure brings forth what is evil.

"And I say to you, that every careless word that men shall speak, they shall render account for it in the day of judgment" (Matt. 12:35–36).

In terse, clear terms Paul adds the fact that "each one of us shall give account of himself to God" (Rom. 14:12).

God doesn't toss His people into a heap and expect them to somehow wind up in glory. He cares about His own. He, in fact, holds us accountable for the way we live. No doubt about it, we'll answer to our Lord. There *will be* vertical accountability. And such accountability will be the basis of our heavenly rewards (2 Cor. 5:10).

But accountability doesn't stop here, it also applies horizontally.

Let love be without hypocrisy. Abhor what is evil; cling to what is good.

Be devoted to one another in brotherly love; give preference to one another in honor; not lagging behind in diligence, fervent in spirit, serving the Lord; rejoicing in hope, persevering in tribulation, devoted to prayer, contributing to the needs of the saints, practicing hospitality.

Bless those who persecute you; bless and curse not. Rejoice with those who rejoice, and weep with those who weep.

Be of the same mind toward one another; do not be haughty in mind, but associate with the lowly. Do not be wise in your own estimation (Rom. 12:9–16).

Now we who are strong ought to bear the weaknesses of those without strength and not just please ourselves.

Let each of us please his neighbor for his good, to his edification.

And concerning you, my brethren, I myself also am convinced that you yourselves are full of goodness, filled with all knowledge, and able also to admonish one another (Rom. 15:1–2,14).

We are not islands of independence, living lives free of one another. We are made to relate, to blend into one another, to touch one another, to answer to one another.

In her fine little book *Up with Worship*, Anne Ortlund uses a splendid word picture to communicate this very point.

> Every congregation has a choice to be one of two things. You can choose to be a bag of marbles, single units that don't affect each other except in collision. On Sunday morning you can choose to go to church or to sleep in: who really cares whether there are 192 or 193 marbles in a bag?
>
> Or you can choose to be a bag of grapes. The juices begin to mingle, and there is no way to extricate yourselves if you tried. Each is part of all. Part of the fragrance. Part of the "stuff."[2]

Sometimes we "grapes" really bleed and hurt. At such times it is not God's desire that we tighten our belts and plow right on. Remember 1 Corinthians 12:26–27?

> And if one member suffers, all the members suffer with it; if one member is honored, all the members rejoice with it.
>
> Now you are Christ's body, and individually members of it.

And what about those occasions when fellow members fall into a slump and begin to walk in a carnal manner, operating their lives from the realm of the flesh instead of the Spirit? Again, do we ignore them and shrug it off thinking, "Well, that's none of my business." No, we are given some explicit biblical counsel regarding this.

> If we live by the Spirit, let us also walk by the Spirit.
>
> Let us not become boastful, challenging one another, envying one another.
>
> Brethren, even if a man is caught in any trespass, you who are spiritual, restore such a one in a spirit of gentleness; each one looking to yourself, lest you too be tempted.
>
> Bear one another's burdens, and thus fulfill the law of Christ (Gal. 5:25–26; 6:1–2).

Unlike the sign on delicate pieces of china in a gift shop, God directs us—*"Please Touch."* For sure, we do need to handle with care, but the worst thing we can do is pass by our brother's or sister's carnality as if it's of no concern to us.

Who can say how many Christians who have defected could have been rescued and restored had someone been honest enough to step in and assist them back to decency and godliness? Ideally, we would hope the person would want help . . . but not all do. Those who choose to be accountable have the greatest hope of change.

One experienced author-counselor writes:

> . . . Behavioral sciences in recent years have expounded the simple truth that "behavior that is observed changes." People who are accountable by their own choice to a group of friends, to a therapy group, to a psychiatrist or a pastoral counselor, to a study group or prayer group, are people who are serious about changing their behavior, and they are finding that change is possible.
>
> Studies done in factories have proven that both quality and quantity of work increase when the employees know that they are being observed. If only God knows what I am doing, since I know He won't tell, I tend to make all kinds of excuses for myself. But if I must report to another or a group of others, I begin to monitor my behavior. If someone is keeping an eye on me, my behavior improves.[3]

When we are in need, people to whom we are closely accountable can come up close and support us. If we begin to drift and stray off course, those same people are there to restore us. Congregations that implement such principles don't have too many in the flock drop out of sight unnoticed or uncared for.

I have never known of one person who has some deep need to ask for some cassette tape to listen to. They want flesh-and-blood people. Take the case of a young couple who began attending our church in recent months. Acting on my counsel from the pulpit that people get involved with each other beyond the worship service, they decided to visit one of our adult fellowships.

During the first visit to the class, a member pulled the couple aside to describe in detail the supportive nature of the class—how they minister to each other in practical ways when needs arise.

That very week the husband suffered a serious accident at his work. He fell from a scaffolding on an oil rig and crushed his spine. After the initial shock, his wife wondered who might be able to help. She thought of the group they had visited on Sunday and found in her purse the name and number of one of the ladies who had invited her to a women's meeting of the class. She called the woman.

After being called, the woman in the class immediately contacted a class officer who got a prayer chain going of about eighty people. Food and baby-sitting were offered so that the wife could spend time with her husband at the hospital. A ministry of encouragement was activated within an hour of the initial phone call.

The husband was hospitalized for an extended period of time. Some feeling has returned to his legs and there is hope that he will eventually walk again. In the meantime, he and his family are surrounded by a group of Christians who are expressing God's love in many practical ways.

By being accountable and in touch, the couple found a whole group of people ready to help.

Positive and Negative

There is another dimension in all this, which we might call the positive-negative experiences connected with accountability. With this in mind, let's take a look at the wisdom of Proverbs.

1. *By being accountable, we are less likely to stumble into a trap.*

> Through presumption comes nothing but strife,
> But with those who receive counsel is wisdom (Prov. 13:10).

> The teaching of the wise is a fountain of life,
> To turn aside from the snares of death (Prov. 13:14).

Poverty and shame will come to him who neglects discipline,
But he who regards reproof will be honored (Prov. 13:18).

He who walks with wise men will be wise,
But the companion of fools will suffer harm (Prov. 13:20).

He whose ear listens to the life-giving reproof
Will dwell among the wise (Prov. 15:31).

He who neglects discipline despises himself,
But he who listens to reproof acquires understanding (Prov. 15:32).

Oil and perfume make the heart glad,
So a man's counsel is sweet to his friend (Prov. 27:9).

Iron sharpens iron,
So one man sharpens another (Prov. 27:17).

As in water face reflects face,
So the heart of man reflects man (Prov. 27:19).

There are snares and unseen reefs beneath the surface of our own independent perception. We all have blind spots. That includes you, too. Wise are those who place themselves in the secure and objective sphere of others' care.

2. *By being accountable, we don't get away with unwise and sinful actions.*

Faithful are the wounds of a friend,
But deceitful are the kisses of an enemy (Prov. 27:6).

Stripes that wound scour away evil,
And strokes reach the innermost parts (Prov. 20:30).

Not even the so-called "superstars" have a corner on life. They, too, are (*especially?*) fallible and subject to blind spots of pride and of failure to carry out their own admonitions to others.

Paul reproved Peter for his hypocrisy.

But when Cephas came to Antioch, I opposed him to his face, because he stood condemned.

For prior to the coming of certain men from James, he used to eat with the Gentiles; but when they came, he began to withdraw and hold himself aloof, fearing the party of the circumcision (Gal. 2:11–12).

Samuel had the unhappy task of confronting Saul:

Then Samuel said to Saul, "Wait, and let me tell you what the Lord said to me last night." And he said to him, "Speak!"

And Samuel said, "Is it not true, though you were little in your own eyes, you were made the head of the tribes of Israel? And the Lord anointed you king over Israel, and the Lord sent you on a mission, and said, 'Go and utterly destroy the sinners, the Amalekites, and fight against them until they are exterminated.'

"Why then did you not obey the voice of the Lord, but rushed upon the spoil and did what was evil in the sight of the Lord?"

Then Saul said to Samuel, "I did obey the voice of the Lord, and went on the mission on which the Lord sent me, and have brought back Agag the king of Amalek, and have utterly destroyed the Amalekites.

"But the people took some of the spoil, sheep and oxen, the choicest of the things devoted to destruction to sacrifice to the Lord your God at Gilgal."

And Samuel said, "Has the Lord as much delight in burnt offerings and sacrifices as in obeying the voice of the Lord? Behold, to obey is better than sacrifice. And to heed than the fat of rams.

"For rebellion is as the sin of divination, and insubordination is as iniquity and idolatry. Because you have rejected the word of the Lord, He has also rejected you from being king" (1 Sam. 15:16–23).

David admitted that such times of affliction and internal bruising were beneficial.

Before I was afflicted I went astray, but now I keep Thy word. . . .

> It is good for me that I was afflicted, that I may learn Thy statutes. . . .
>
> I know, O Lord, that Thy judgments are righteous, and that in faithfulness Thou hast afflicted me (Ps. 119:67,71,75).

As I said at the beginning of this chapter, when I'm tempted to fudge at a traffic signal, there's that letter to haunt me! That is precisely the kind of thing David had in mind.

FOUR PRACTICAL SUGGESTIONS

Now that we have come to an understanding of what accountability is and isn't . . . and since we have ample support from Scripture that it is not only valid but, in fact, vital, let's finalize the issue by thinking through several practical suggestions for implementation.

1. *Stop and consider the value of becoming accountable.* Personalize this suggestion by using "I," "me," "my."

- Like everyone else, I have blind spots. By being accountable, I will gain insight I don't have in myself.
- Because I lack sufficient strength and wisdom to cope with pressure, temptation, and pride all on my own, I need others near me.
- The kind of world I live in has too many booby traps and subtle snares for me to handle on my own (especially when I travel . . . or when I'm all alone). I need additional strength.

2. *Ask yourself two questions.* Asking is easy, but answering them may hurt.

- Why do I remain isolated and unaccountable?
- What if I stay in this condition?

If you are in the category of a highly visible leader, a much-respected pastor, a Christian entertainer, a speaker who is often on the road, a media personality, I *plead* with you. The adversary has you in the cross wires of his scope. His darts are pointed in your direction. Your hope of survival, your means of escaping the traps, is largely connected with your willingness to place yourself within the circle of a few friends *outside* your family. I urge you to do this soon.

3. *Choose at least one other person (preferably two or three) with whom you will meet regularly.* They need to be *very* carefully chosen. These are some traits to look for:

- Confidentiality (if married, that person's mate must have the same trait).
- Honesty (someone who is not in awe of you).
- Authenticity (free from hypocrisy, sincere).
- Objectivity (won't always agree with you or tell you what you want to hear).
- Godliness (you respect their walk with God—each is definitely a Christian).
- Availability (accessible, able to meet within a short notice).
- Loyalty (faithful, staying power, consistent).

4. *Develop a relationship that strengthens your grip on spiritual things.*

I'm not talking about a business consultant or a financial counselor, helpful as those may be. Nor am I talking about a professional therapist who may help you work through your emotional struggles. This individual with whom you meet is one who helps "encourage you in God" (1 Sam. 23:16) as Jonathan did with David. It is your spiritual sensitivity that needs monitoring and appraisal.

I'll not linger much longer (this chapter has almost become a book unto itself), but I cannot close without mentioning once again that one of the best decisions I ever made several years ago was to seek out several men I respected who would meet with me, pray, talk, evaluate, counsel, weigh decisions, assist me in keeping my head together and make sure my heart was right before God. They are honest with me, open, affirming yet not gullible, tactful yet confronting, good listeners yet wise counselors.

God has used them to show me some of the traps I would have missed and to alter my course when I was moving in the wrong direction. Words fail to describe the benefits I have reaped—actually we have reaped together—as a result of having them near.

If only they could do something about my driving habits; but then, they're only human. Some things can only be dealt with by prayer and fasting!

DISCUSSION IDEAS AND QUESTIONS

- Define accountability in your own words. Give some examples of what you believe it includes.
- Can you remember the two dangerous extremes? Talk about them. Have you ever witnessed or been the recipient of either? Share what you went through at the time.
- Discuss the difference between necessary and healthy privacy and unwise isolationism. How can a person tell if he or she is moving from the former to the latter?
- A great deal of chapter 11 was a presentation of the biblical justification of accountability. Choose a passage or two that clarified an issue or encouraged you and share your thoughts.
- Turn back to Proverbs 27:6. Dig into it with others in the group. Try your hand at your own paraphrase. Name one specific way in which the verse helps you.
- The chapter closes with four practical suggestions. Review them orally. Talk them over. Are you willing to put each suggestion to use in your life?
- Pick a particular individual you really admire, perhaps some high-profile leader whom God has used in your life. Pray for him or her. As you pray, work your way through the four suggestions and ask the Lord to protect your leader-friend from the subtle traps of our adversary, the devil.

12

A Hope Transplant:
The Essential Operation

CHURCHES ARE LIKE CHILDREN. They come in different shapes and sizes, personalities and styles. No two are exactly alike.

In the process of well over two decades of preaching and ministering, I have had the opportunity to be in all kinds of churches. The variety has been nothing short of remarkable. While traveling late last summer, I sat down and drew up a list of the different types, sort of a cross-section sampling of churches where I have visited and ministered. Here's what it looked like:

- Extremely conservative and theologically buttoned-up-tight style.
- Fairly liberal, what I'd call theologically loosey-goosey style.
- Highly emotional, informal, answer-back congregations.
- Absolutely silent, stoic, straight, and stern.
- Biblically illiterate . . . not a Bible within gunshot distance.

- Well-taught, in fact, almost a classroom atmosphere.
- Some have been large, a few *huge* with multiple balconies.
- Others were tiny, only a handful meeting in a home.
- Old, I mean hundreds of years old.
- A few less than a month in existence.
- Some were English-speaking . . . others called for translators.

I've preached in black churches where I thought we'd never finish the service! There were three offerings, over an hour of music, lengthy times of prayer, and two full-length sermons (emphasis on length) both from me and the pastor. I left the place dripping wet and hoarse. I don't think I've had so much fun since "the hogs ate my little brother." I mean, when those folks say "Amen" to a preacher, it's like saying "sic 'em" to a bulldog. And then I've preached in other places where a twenty-minute sermon was considered a marathon. Those places usually have weird-looking pulpits, by the way.

Some churches where I've been loved music. They had a full orchestra, over one hundred in the choir, a lovely pipe organ, and employed music as a beautiful enhancement to worship. While others didn't believe in using musical instruments. Everything was a cappella. A few were highly cultured and sophisticated "clubs" where elegance and scholarship were the passwords of entrance, and others were dirt poor. I remember one place that requested that I wear cutoffs and a T-shirt (in California, naturally). Once they saw my knees and legs, they were sorry they had made that request.

I've spoken in churches torn by strife (several splits in their brief history) and others that have hung together for decades, unified and still excited about the Lord. One has had the same pastor for over forty years, and when you consider that the average minister stays only three to five years, then moves on, the man who remains *that* long today is a phenomenon. Some churches were more like entertainment centers than houses of worship; whereas, others were as plain and unimaginative as a weather-beaten clapboard barn. One in particular resembled a cinder block fortress—square corners, no windows, cement floors, hard pews, an upright piano, naked lightbulbs hanging from long wires, and a flat ceiling. I couldn't imagine being sentenced to the place. The echo, however, allowed everyone to hear the sermon twice, so nobody ever left feeling cheated.

I have not exaggerated. Some churches were so winsome and warm that I never wanted to leave. Others were so scary that I'm still trying to believe they actually exist. Whoever doesn't think God has a sense of humor hasn't seen the churches I've been in.

THE MOST TRAGIC CHURCHES ON EARTH

Two churches stand out, however, as the most tragic of all. Both are urban ministries with a rich, illustrious history. One is located in a dangerous section of an angry, volatile neighborhood. There are wrought-iron bars on the windows, double locks on all the doors (the congregation is actually locked in when they gather for worship), and women are escorted to their cars when the meetings end . . . day or night. The other has a completely different external appearance. Those folks aren't frightened, they are proud. Proud of all the wrong things. From the outside you would think they had it all together, but when you get in and listen and observe, you realize something terribly important is missing. It's what's missing in the other church too. And that is what makes both ministries so tragic.

Interestingly, both places talk of their past. "The Way We Were" would be an appropriate offertory in either church. Great men and women once ministered there. There used to be an aggressive, pace-setting outreach program of evangelism in the community, a broad vision for mission in God's world program, attractive youth ministries, grand and stimulating preaching, an educational program for people from the cradle to the grave, exciting, crowded conditions, discipleship, and concerned people in prayer . . . the whole scene. But no longer. . . . All that is left of the past glory of those two great ministries is a row of pictures hanging in the hallway and the memories in the minds of a few.

It's not so much a problem of what is there as it is a problem of what is missing. That's what makes it so tragic. There is an absence of vitality and power. The folks are not dreaming about tomorrow and seeking God's mind for their future. They're thinking only of the past. They are churches that have lost their *hope*. The Spirit of God is no longer free to move among them, it seems. In that "hopeless" atmosphere it's almost as if He has lifted His presence from those places. It is enough to make you weep. Perhaps Samuel Stevenson who wrote these words *was* weeping:

> A city full of churches
> Great preacher, lettered men,
> Grand music, choirs and organs;
> If these all fail, what then?
> Good workers, eager, earnest,
> Who labour hour by hour;
> But where, oh where, my brother,
> Is God's Almighty power?
>
> Refinement: education!
> They want the very best.
> Their plans and schemes are perfect
> They give themselves no rest;
> They get the best of talent,
> They try their uttermost,
> But what they need, brother,
> Is God the Holy Ghost![1]

What the heart is to your physical body, what morale is to a unit of fighting men, what spirit is to a ball team, hope is to a church. Remove it and you have reduced the place of worship to a morgue with a steeple. An empty shell. A building, perhaps even a lovely external structure housing zombie-like creatures going through the motions of religion but lacking vitality. Sunday meetings are like narcotic fixes to deaden the pain of empty lives. Hope, the prince and power of motivation, has vanished.

That may describe the place where you worship. Perhaps not to the same extreme, but you sense something is missing. You have read these chapters, and you've felt the excitement and challenge of the Hebrews as they left Egypt and struck out for Canaan. You've watched the Red Sea open, you've seen the cloud by day and felt the warmth of the pillar of fire by night. You've witnessed Jericho's walls crumble to the ground. You've marched into Canaan and heard the warnings of Joshua. You've been stirred (as I have) with the realization that drawing closer, being open, dropping your guard, and becoming accountable are all attainable and exciting goals. You want that . . . but when you think about trying it in your church, you lose heart. Maybe you are to the place of thinking, "It may work for others, but it won't at the church I attend." Maybe some of that same hopelessness has colored your thinking and you are about to slam this thing closed with a silent sigh, "It's only a dream." You may be the pastor of a seemingly hopeless church. You are seriously wondering if it is worth the effort. Perhaps the hopelessness has begun to affect your preaching and your leadership.

Before going any further, let me encourage you. It is never too late to start doing what is right! Things may seem without hope, but that's *today.* And that's the *past.* What you have read about open relationships and becoming deeper, closer, and stronger in friendship and love with others can help. It *cannot* hurt. It may be the central catalyst God would use to bring a fresh touch of His Spirit back into your church and its congregation. Take heart, my friend. You could be on the verge of a God-ordained renewal that has the potential of turning your place of ministry right-side up. In light of that, I'd like to transplant hope from the pages of Scripture into your heart and, ultimately, into your place of worship. I spent my first chapter describing how hope was revived in the place where I worship. Now let's spend this final chapter thinking about how it can be implemented where you worship. We've spent enough time talking about individual people; let's think about churches for awhile . . . churches of hope. How can we bring the hope back?

A BRIEF ANALYSIS OF HOPE

We toss around words like *faith* and *love* all the time. And most of us can describe both with minimal difficulty. But *hope?* What in the world is it? And is it really *that* essential?

Description

Webster defines hope, "to desire with expectation of fulfillment." To hope is to anticipate. It is more than dreaming, however. It is possessing within ourselves an expectation that someday there will be the fulfillment of that desire. It will become a reality. Hope always looks to the future, it's always on tiptoes. It keeps us going. It makes a dismal today bearable because it promises a brighter tomorrow. Without hope, something inside all of us dies.

The Greek term translated "hope" means much the same as our English word—"favorable and confident expectation." We can live several weeks without food, days without water, and only minutes without oxygen, but without hope—forget it.

> Take from a man his wealth, and you hinder him; take from him his purpose, and you slow him down. But take from man his hope, and you stop him. He can go on without wealth, and even without purpose, for a while. But he will not go on without hope.[2]

The *Good News Bible* renders Proverbs 13:12: "When hope is crushed, the heart is crushed, But a wish come true fills you with joy."

The New American Standard Bible says: "Hope deferred makes the heart sick, but desire fulfilled is a tree of life." A loss of hope *sickens* the heart. The Hebrew term CHA-LAH (translated "sick") is a word that suggests the idea of being "diseased." When the noun *sickness* is used in reference to a nation, it presents the idea of calamity, grief, or affliction. The term is often used in a severe sense, hence the word picture of the heart being "crushed" is an apt description.

A rather remarkable series of tests and dozens of comprehensive studies have established the fact that hope and survival are inseparably connected.

In an article in *New York* magazine, Douglas Colligan writes of the "Broken Heart" study. This study researched the mortality rate of 4,500 widowers within six months of their wives' deaths. The findings of the study showed that the widowers had a mortality rate 40 percent higher than other men the same age.

In the same article Colligan cites the example of Major F. J. Harold Kushner, who was held by the Viet Cong for five and a half years:

> Among the prisoners in Kushner's POW camp was a tough young marine, 24 years old, who had already survived two years of prison-camp life in relatively good health. Part of the reason for this was that the camp commander had promised to release the man if he cooperated. Since this had been done before with others, the marine turned into a model POW and the leader of the camp's thought-reform group. As time passed he gradually realized that his captors had lied to him. When the full realization of this took hold he became a zombie. He refused to do all work, rejected all offers of food and encouragement, and simply lay on his cot sucking his thumb. In a matter of weeks he was dead.[3]

Philip Yancey in his book *Where Is God When It Hurts?* says "Kushner's experience is a tragic, negative example of the need for some hope to live for."[4]

It is a proven fact that hope must be present or disease sets in. I've seen this in marriages, haven't you? The bride-to-be has her "hope chest" in which she places tangible things and intangible dreams. Her heart beats faster as she opens the chest and anticipates her joys of the future. She marries the man of her dreams. Hope keeps them going as he grinds his way through school. Hope takes them to their first home, through the births of their three children, and into a second home, large enough for their full-size family and a few pets. Then midlife seizes the reins, somehow getting a strangle hold on their hope. She loses some interest, he stops bringing her flowers, they begin to spin in separate orbits. Hope fades. They half-heartedly try to work it out . . . but the disease has taken its toll. As one lady said to me with a sigh, "It wasn't until I lost all hope of recovery that I finally gave up. When the hope vanished, so did my energy. It was all over—the fun, the intimacy, the drive, the dreams, all the stuff that made it stick died."

A Question

Can that happen in a church? Yes. Never overnight, you understand. It's often so imperceptible that you aren't even aware it is happening. If you were, you'd stop it. But it's like erosion—silent, never sudden, yet constant. The good news is that this disease isn't always terminal.

The big question is: What does it take to keep a congregation full of hope? Or, to use other words: How can we keep the disease of hopelessness away? Or, perhaps: What will restore our hope?

I have thought about this a lot. If you recall my words in chapter 1, in our case I became concerned that our size and the sameness of routine, once we got settled in our new facilities, would "steal our enthusiasm" . . . which is another way of saying, "take away our hope." Congregational hope and health go hand in hand.

Some Ways to Keep Hope Strong

While thinking about how to fan the flame of hope in a church, I came across the first letter Peter wrote. Since he was the one so intimately involved in the first-century congregation at Jerusalem, he should offer some guidelines or ideas worth duplicating today. When I arrived at the fifth chapter of that letter, things began to fall into place. No less than five realistic suggestions seemed to stand out. Each one is an ingredient found in churches I'm aware of today who are getting the job done . . . each one enhances hope.

The Right Kind of Leadership

> Therefore, I exhort the elders among you, as your fellow elder and witness of the sufferings of Christ, and a partaker also of the glory that is to be revealed, shepherd the flock of God among you, not under compulsion, but voluntarily, according to the will of God; and not for sordid gain, but with eagerness; nor yet as lording it over those allotted to your charge, but proving to be examples to the flock (1 Pet. 5:1–4).

Those dear people were slugging it out in a tough time when persecution, misunderstanding, even martyrdom were grim realities. Therefore, we shouldn't be surprised that Peter speaks first to those in leadership. If hope leaves the heart of the leader, it isn't long before the entire congregation follows suit. Naturally, they need his initial words of counsel.

Take a close look at the verses you just read. See the contrasts? They follow the strong imperative, "shepherd the flock!" But how? What should characterize those who serve as shepherds of God's flock? Let me diagram it for you:

Not . . . (negatively)	But . . . (positively)
. . . under compulsion	. . . voluntarily
. . . for sordid gain	. . . with eagerness
. . . lording it over	. . . being an example

The same old nemesis awaits all who serve local congregations, regardless of the era or geography: silver, sloth, and self! Those who desire to cultivate a close, unguarded, deeply committed congregation must come to terms with each of these three temptations. There are stories—some of them almost too frightening to believe—which have come to my attention, stories of pastors who are "in it for the money" . . . who have long since lost the joy of ministry (and there are hundreds of joys!) . . . who are so insecure they must dominate and browbeat the congregation. These leaders should not be surprised that hope is fading in their congregations.

For flocks to flourish they need acceptance, freedom, love, lots of reinforcement, regular nourishment, room to fail, an atmosphere of expectation, and true enthusiasm. This is true for young and old alike, for singles and marrieds, for women and men, for the cultured and refined as well as those with limited interests, for blue collar and white collar workers, for Democrats and Republicans. Regardless of color and with no concern for financial status, they are all God's flock, not the pastor's people. They belong to Him, not the preacher or the pastoral staff. They want to be challenged to think. They need to know it's okay to disagree, to ask questions, to hold other opinions. Yes, and even to fuss (most already know that). They have to have the freedom to laugh, to respond, to serve, to weep, to be completely who they are . . . and they get their cues from their leader.

Uptight, intense, superdefensive, easily threatened leaders do not spawn congregations of close, caring, relaxed, accepting, completely human, and believable relationships. If the congregation senses that their leader's "example to the flock" is all these things and more of the same, they will have all the green lights they need to proceed. But if they witness that the most important thing to him is biblical instruction (almost to the exclusion of much else) they will begin to be instructors. If he is harsh and rigid, they will be too. If he always has to be right, they put great emphasis on who's right and who's wrong. If he likes to exhort and put down, so will they. The style and "flavor" of a church come from those in leadership. As is always true, right leadership results in maximum benefits.

True Humility toward One Another

Peter goes on to say:

> You younger men, likewise, be subject to your elders; and all of you, clothe yourselves with humility toward one another, for God is opposed to the proud, but gives grace to the humble.
>
> Humble yourselves, therefore, under the mighty hand of God, that He may exalt you at the proper time (1 Pet. 5:5–6).

There's a beautiful balance here, isn't there? Younger men are encouraged to listen to the older gentlemen. There is cross-generational respect and free communication. But does this suggest the older guys have a corner on truth? Is this some kind of king-of-the-hill power play? Hardly. Peter goes on to say that *all* of them (older, mid-adults, teens, young singles, older singles, children, parents, pastors, elders, ushers, you name it) were to wear the same garment. What is it? Is it biblical accuracy? As important and valuable as that is, no, that's not the garment everybody in the congregation is to wear. Nor is it education. Nor wealth. Nor poverty. It is one of those absolutely essential ingredients that assure everyone it is safe to drop your guard—humility. Pride kills openness! With that in mind, there are more murders in churches than any other place in the world.

How does God respond to pride? Verse 6 says He *opposes* it. Peter uses a strong battle term here. Pride calls out God's armies. It brings in His heavy artillery. On more than one place in Scripture we read He flat out *hates* pride. Why? What's the big deal?

- Pride creates an "exclusive club" mentality in churches.
- Pride resists sharing, making room for the stronger, those who may be different than most.
- Pride stops innovation and change.
- Pride always has to have the answers. The definite article is terribly important to pride.
- Pride is dogmatic, unteachable, closed-minded.

That's why God hates it. That's why churches who have hope are comprised of folks who wear the garment of humility. God exalts us "at the proper time" if we wear the right clothing— a teachable spirit, vulnerability, approachability toward one another.

There's a third ingredient we don't want to forget.

Release of Anxiety

For release of anxiety what better advice than 1 Peter 5:7, "casting all your anxiety upon Him, because He cares for you!"

Worry robs us of hope. It immobilizes the body of Christ by reminding us of all the things that are wrong and bad and threatening. Worry suffocates us, pushing our heads under the water of all our troubles and trials.

A worried church doesn't risk. It reacts. Instead of staying on the cutting edge, it retreats and adopts a fight-back mentality. It spends less time dreaming and more time defending. An anxious congregation is more aware of what's wrong in the world than what's right with the Lord.

Have you spent much time with worry-warts in the Christian ranks? They look like they've been baptized in lemon juice. Anxiety-prone people carry burdens; they don't cast them off. And the longer folks do that the "stranger" they get—the more paranoid, the less joyful. Some become self-styled "prophets" who get a little wide-eyed and fanatical with doomsday declarations, have you noticed? And they seem to feed on congregations that are growing and excited. They're attracted to churches on the move. I agree with the wag who first observed this and shrugged, "Where there's light, there are bugs!"

In every church there are enough problems to make any pastor an emotional basket case. Parking problems. Vandalism. Gossip. Wayward and carnal Christians. Neighborhood complaints. Sickness. Bad marriages. Financial woes. Staff disharmony. Poor location. Loud traffic outside. Lack of forgiveness, "Get rid of the pastor" talk. You name it, some churches have it in spades.

By the way, I just heard of a super way to get rid of your pastor! C'mon, it's time for a laugh. There's this new chain letter going around among churches. No cost is involved. You just send a copy of the letter to six other churches that are tired of their ministers too. Then you bundle up your pastor and ship him to the church at the bottom of the list. In one week you will receive in return 16,436 ministers . . . one of whom should be a dandy! But beware, one church broke the chain and got their old minister back.

You see, there are any number of creative ways to break with the anxiety syndrome. The best is still "casting all your anxiety upon Him."

An Alert and Discerning Awareness of the Adversary

Churches that stay healthy and full of hope, vision, and enthusiasm possess a keen awareness of the enemy. See how Peter deals with this?

> Be of sober spirit, be on the alert. Your adversary, the devil, prowls about like a roaring lion, seeking someone to devour.
>
> But resist him, firm in your faith, knowing that the same experiences of suffering are being accomplished by your brethren who are in the world (1 Pet. 5:8–9).

To be "sober" is to be strong, stable, self-controlled.

To be "on the alert" is to be watchful, aware.

Those are our commands, fellow Christians. Orders from headquarters. We are in no fun-'n-games, carefree work, you know. There's an enemy on the loose. And whether or not we are aware of him (we *should* be!), he is certainly aware of us. He knows us thoroughly. He is crafty, brilliant, experienced, and resilient in combat. And he despises whatever represents God and whoever is carrying out God's work. Since he is on the prowl and dedicated to our defeat, we are to be mindful of this and not deceived into thinking he couldn't care less. The truth is that he couldn't care more!

Look again at his objective: to *devour*. I'd call that an aggressive strategy, wouldn't you? He will stop at nothing. If a strategy to attack from without doesn't work, he will use an internal maneuver—other people, alien thoughts, wild imagination, some caustic comment, a season of low-grade depression, an unexplainable series of events, and I might add *apathy*. Yes, plain old indifference, passive unconcern.

And what does a church do under such attacks? Resist! Resist! Resist! Stand firm in faith!! I have found it to be helpful if I acknowledge an awareness of his presence to other Christians. If there is one tactic the adversary cannot abide, it's exposure.

We were going through a difficult time in our church a few months ago. Many were not aware of the intensity nor was it appropriate for me to announce it. I was struggling. I could not get on top. For the life of me, I was unable to unravel the whole thing and reach some kind of conclusion. My lack of decisiveness irritated me and there were other noticeable problems created in the fallout of the whole episode. I became preoccupied. My leadership faltered. I began to withdraw, pull in, get quiet, and lie low. Not being the low-lying type, I couldn't continue in that posture. Finally, in a conversation with a man I've admired for years, he made a comment that put everything in proper perspective. After listening for ten or fifteen minutes, he said, "Sounds like a satanic attack to me, Chuck. I mean, if he can get his foot into the door of your life and get you intimidated and full of doubt and waiting for the next shoe to fall, he's won a massive victory. Just think of the lives that are affected if your leadership begins to falter." It clicked. I was amazed to think I had failed to realize I wasn't wrestling against mere flesh and blood. No way! The prowler had found a weak spot and was making his moves. What a difference once we become aware of his insidious and deceptive strategies!

Thus far, we've considered four ways to keep hope revived and alive in our lives and churches. Peter mentions one more:

Respond Well to Adversity

> And after you have suffered for a little while, the God of all grace, who called you to His eternal glory in Christ, will Himself perfect, confirm, strengthen and establish you.
>
> To Him be dominion forever and ever. Amen (1 Pet. 5:10–11).

How easy to fall prey to self-pity! It is the most natural and acceptable response to suffering. In fact, people will often encourage it in us! Peter takes a different stance. He realizes his readers are in the trenches. It's not a matter of will they suffer, but how much more can they endure?

Interestingly, he refuses to focus on their hardship and affliction. He immediately jumps to the benefits—"After you have suffered—God will. . . ." What *great* perspective! He refuses to get all bogged down in the pain of it all. He turns their (and our) attention to the end results.

Churches that have hope take a hitch in their belts when the going gets rough. They stand instead of shrink. They realize this temporary test will reap permanent benefits. To use a runner's term, they "lean into the wind" rather than give up and surrender to it.

Look at the benefits. God will:

- Perfect: This term carries with it the idea of repairing weak or broken parts.
- Confirm: To make firm, solid as granite, tough as fiber, strong as tempered steel.
- Strengthen: Take away the flab, replace fragility with stability.
- Establish: This is the idea of laying down a foundation. Suffering drives us back to the bedrock of our faith.

It's time for more people to talk straight about how we view pain and problems. I've read and heard enough to know that

we are viewing it all wrong! I realize that's a sweeping generaliza-
tion, but I'm convinced that it's true. We have become masters
of explanation in this generation. Everything now has its label
and we quickly look for such when something happens, especially
something that brings discomfort. Instead of anticipating the
positive ramifications of the affliction, we settle into our martyr
mentality, we look for pity and are resentful when we don't
find it. Rather than adopt a victor's stance (this will be beneficial,
this is no unfair accident of fate, "God is in this"), we resort
to the pathetic wail of a victim ("Why? Woe is me. If only
people knew how bad I've got it. Will it ever end?").

You see, hope dies with that kind of thinking. It is crushed
beneath the load of our self-appointed misery. Problems do not
go away. They must be worked through or else they remain
forever a barrier to the growth and development of our spirit.
And we pass much of this kind of thinking on to our children.
How much better to teach (and to model) a determination that
refuses to quit when we encounter the pain that conflicts and
events bring our way. Carl Jung was correct, "Neurosis is always
a substitute for legitimate suffering."[5]

In an excellent book that tracks this view in great detail, *The
Road Less Traveled*, the author boldly declares:

> . . . it is in this whole process of meeting and solving problems
> that life has its meaning. Problems are the cutting edge that distin-
> guishes between success and failure. Problems call forth our cour-
> age and our wisdom; indeed, they create our courage and our
> wisdom. It is only because of problems that we grow mentally
> and spiritually. When we desire to encourage the growth of the
> human spirit, we challenge and encourage the human capacity
> to solve problems, just as in school we deliberately set problems
> for our children to solve. It is through the pain of confronting
> and resolving problems that we learn. As Benjamin Franklin said,
> "Those things that hurt, instruct." It is for this reason that wise
> people learn not to dread but actually to welcome problems and
> actually to welcome the pain of problems.
>
> Most of us are not so wise. Fearing the pain involved, almost
> all of us, to a greater or lesser degree, attempt to avoid problems.

We procrastinate, hoping that they will go away. We ignore them, forget them, pretend they do not exist. We even take drugs to assist us in ignoring them, so that by deadening ourselves to the pain we can forget the problems that cause the pain. We attempt to skirt around problems rather than meet them head on. We attempt to get rid of them rather than suffer through them.

This tendency to avoid problems and the emotional suffering inherent in them is the primary basis of all human mental illness.[6]

A Closing Comment

I would suggest that you take the time to review each of Peter's five suggestions for keeping hope strong, especially if you are serious about inculcating some workable ideas into your life and into your church. It has been my observation that things don't suddenly or automatically change externally . . . they shift and move around first in our heads, in there where we turn ideas over, where we plant the seeds that later grow into action.

If developing open relationships in your life and in your church is something that you consider worth all the effort, be ready for a challenge. In my opinion it is the best way to survive on this lonely, busy planet, and it is worth whatever risk it requires. The alternative is no longer an option to me.

DISCUSSION IDEAS AND QUESTIONS

- Spend a while talking about your church. Do some evaluating. What is it that you appreciate most? What are the ministries that appeal to your family members? If you brought a visitor next Sunday, what do you think would leave the greatest impression?
- Where are you able to make the greatest contribution in your church? What ministry would interest you the most? Talk about why.
- Is hope lagging or flourishing in your church? Go back and read again the description of hope in chapter 12. Is it possible that you could help strengthen the hope of your church? How?
- Go around the room and each person read a verse from 1 Peter 5:1–11. Now, taking the five suggestions for strengthening the hope of a church, discuss them together. Try to be specific as you honestly imagine *your* church in light of Peter's words.
- Pain is an inescapable reality in life. As we saw at the end of the chapter, affliction and hardship may be tough to bear, but they bring marvelous benefits and depth of character. Share one or two things you have learned in the crucible.
- Before leaving, give God thanks for teaching you these lessons you learned in the furnace of affliction.

Conclusion

IT WAS BACK IN 1981 that I decided to write a book on servant-hood. The result was *Improving Your Serve,* a volume dedicated to the art of unselfish living. As time passed and the publisher informed me of its success, I was encouraged to write a second with a similar-sounding title but completely different in content. That was 1982, the year *Strengthening Your Grip* was released. As you who read it will remember, it is a book about some of the essentials we need to get a grip on in this aimless world of ours. I considered those two would surely be sufficient—sort of a one-two punch to help a few folks who are trying to stay on their feet in this wild 'n woolly generation.

Before 1983 had dawned, however, my friends at Word Books were back for round three (no, this isn't a fifteen-round bout), telling me "a trilogy would be appreciated" since the first and second books had been met with such approval by the general public, Christian and non-Christian alike. Hence, *Dropping Your Guard* has found its way into your hands. As you know by now, this has been another kind of book entirely, quite distinct from either of the first two.

The content of the first was primarily directed to those who wish to assist others in the family of God. The second looked more into the world and addressed pertinent issues that are up for grabs in our fast-paced society. But this one looks within. This volume talks about you and me, down deep inside. It explores and exposes our tendency to protect ourselves . . . even though we may not realize we are doing so.

> Most of us can't see how we have become protective. We prefer to see ourselves as open and gentle; it may be shocking to hear that others—especially those closest to us—may see us as hard, critical, and closed. . . .
>
> To paraphrase the poet: "How do I protect myself? Let me count the ways."[1]

This book encourages our dropping all those protective guards. It appeals for the value of open relationships. It says, in effect, be who you are, let the truth be known, come on . . . open up . . . let's not mask the truth any longer.

Of the three, this one is the most personal. Even though you didn't invite me to do so, I have taken the liberty to probe within you, helping you search for and discover some clues that might explain why you have opted for isolation instead of openness.

Now the work begins. With the period at the end of this conclusion, theory stops and reality starts. The gauge of this book's effectiveness will not be measured by how much you've marked in it or by whether you quote from it, but rather by the extent to which you put it to the test.

You see, if you really believe these things are valuable, if you are convinced that being unprotected and open is better than being somebody else behind a mask, you will start living that way. You will take the risk. And I've got great news for you—

someday you will discover you are not able to live any other way. Living without masks is addictive. It's also terribly contagious.

It makes me smile when I think of the benefits that you will begin to enjoy as you lift the truth from these printed pages and transfer it into your talk and your walk. Think of the difference in your home, where you work, at your church, with your friends! Think of the relief you will feel from removing all those thick and phony masks that have plagued you for years!

Okay, my friend, toss this thing aside. You've read about it enough. You don't need more theoretical information. What you need is practical exposure . . . a lifetime to do what you say you believe.

So what are you waiting for? Get out there and dare to be authentic, whole, uniquely who you are. You're in for the time of your life!

Notes

Chapter 1. Loosening the Mask: How It All Began

1. Bernard Berelson and Gary A. Steiner, *Human Behavior: An Inventory of Scientific Findings* (New York: Harcourt, Brace & World, 1964), 252.

2. "Mobility," *Society,* 14 (Jan./Feb. 1977): 9. Published by permission of Transaction, Inc. from *Society,* vol. 14, #2. Copyright © 1977 by Transaction, Inc. See also Robert Kanigel, "Stay-Put Americans," *Human Behavior,* May 1979.

3. U.S. Bureau of Labor Statistics, *Monthly Labor Review* (October 1963):1145 and (December 1979):48. This trend, which reversed that for the period 1951–63, reflects at least in part the growing proportion of young workers, whose job tenure is much shorter than that of older Americans.

4. Vance Packard, *A Nation of Strangers* (New York: David McKay, 1972), 270.

5. Mildred Newman and Bernard Berkowitz, *How to Be Your Own Best Friend* (New York: Random House, 1971), 7. Used by permission.

6. From Bruce Larson, *There's a Lot More to Health Than Not Being Sick,* copyright © 1981, pp. 59–60; used by permission of Word Books, Publisher, Waco, Texas 76796.

7. Charles R. Swindoll, *People of Refuge,* a film produced by Word, Inc., Waco, Texas, 1982.

Chapter 2. Digging Deeper, Risking Change

1. Amy Carmichael, *If* (Montreal: Christian Literature Crusade [n.d.]), 48. Taken from copyrighted material; used by permission of the Christian Literature Crusade, Fort Washington, PA 19034.

Chapter 3. Getting Closer, Growing Stronger

1. From John Donne, *Devotions,* XVII, as quoted in *Familiar Quotations,* ed. John Bartlett (Boston: Little, Brown and Company, 1955), 218.

2. Charles Paul Conn, *Making It Happen* (Old Tappan, NJ: Fleming H. Revell Co., 1981), 95.

3. Alan Loy McGinnis, *The Friendship Factor* (Minneapolis: Augsburg Publishing House, 1979), 20. Reprinted by permission from *The Friendship Factor* by Alan Loy McGinnis, copyright 1979 Augsburg Publishing House.

4. Ibid., 60–61.

Chapter 4. Operation Assimilation

1. From *Hide or Seek* by James Dobson, copyright © 1974, 1979 by Fleming H. Revell Co., pp. 133, 134. Published by Fleming H. Revell Co. Used by permission.

2. *Webster's New Collegiate Dictionary* (Springfield, MA: G. & C. Merriam Company, 1980), 67.

3. John Naisbitt, *Megatrends* (New York: Warner Books, 1982), 53.

4. From Tom J. Fatjo, Jr., and Keith Miller, *With No Fear of Failure*, copyright © 1981, p. 16; used by permission of Word Books, Publisher, Waco, Texas 76796.

5. Leslie B. Flynn, *Great Church Fights* (Wheaton, IL: Victor Books, A Division of SP Publications, Inc., 1976), 44. Used by permission of the author.

6. *The Los Angeles Times*, 9 May 1983, Orange County Edition, Sec. CC††/Part II, p. 1.

7. Excerpted from *We Really Do Need Each Other* by Reuben Welch (pp. 110–111). Copyright © 1976 by Impact Books, A Division of John T. Benson Publishing Company. Reassigned to the Zondervan Corporation, 1982. Used by permission.

Chapter 5. United and Invincible

1. "The Bond of Love" by Otis Skillings, © 1971 by Lillenas Publishing Co. All rights reserved. Used by permission.

2. From pp. 90–91, 93 from *Life Together* by Dietrich Bonhoeffer, tr. by John W. Doberstein, copyright © 1954 by Harper & Row Publishers, Inc. and used by permission of the publisher.

3. Theodore H. Epp, *Elijah: A Man of Like Nature* (Lincoln, NB: The Good News Broadcasting Association, Inc., 1965), 63.

4. Alan Loy McGinnis, *The Friendship Factor* (Minneapolis, MN: Augsburg Publishing House, 1979), 179–180. Reprinted by permission from *The Friendship Factor* by Alan Loy McGinnis, copyright 1979 Augsburg Publishing House.

Chapter 6. When the Fellowship Breaks Down

1. Taken from *Fearfully and Wonderfully Made* by Paul Brand, M.D., with Philip Yancey (pp. 59–60). Copyright ©

1980 by Dr. Paul Brand and Philip Yancey. Used by permission of Zondervan Publishing House.

2. Mouton Chambers, *Leadership*, A Publication of *Christianity Today*, vol. 2, no. 3 (summer 1981): 80.

3. Leslie B. Flynn, *Great Church Fights* (Wheaton, IL: Victor Books, A Division of SP Publications, 1976), 91. Used by permission of the author.

Chapter 7. Authentic Love

1. Hal David and Burt Bacharach, "What the World Needs Now" (Los Angeles, CA: Blue Seas Music Publishers & Jac Music, Inc., 1965). Lyric by Hal David; music by Burt Bacharach. Copyright © 1965 Blue Seas Music, Inc. and Jac Music Company, Inc. International copyright secured. Made in USA. All rights reserved.

2. *The Friendless American Male* by David W. Smith. © Copyright 1983, Regal Books, Ventura, CA 93006. Used by permission.

3. Reprinted from *Men: A Book for Women* (p. 165), edited by James Wagenvoord. Copyright © 1978 by Product Development International Holding, n.v. Reprinted by permission of Avon Books, New York.

4. Alan Loy McGinnis, *The Friendship Factor* (Minneapolis: Augsburg Publishing House, 1979), 48–49. Reprinted by permission from *The Friendship Factor* by Alan Loy McGinnis, copyright 1979 Augsburg Publishing House.

Chapter 8. Needed: Shelter for Storm Victims

1. From Bruce Larson and Keith Miller, *The Edge of Adventure*, copyright © 1974, p. 156; used by permission of Word Books, Publisher, Waco, Texas 76796.

2. From *Psalms of My Life* by Joseph Bayly (p. 16). Published by Tyndale House Publishers, Inc., © 1969. Used by permission.

3. Taken from *Christ in Isaiah* by F. B. Meyer (p. 9), made and printed in Great Britain by Purnell and Sons, Ltd. Paulton (Somerset) and London. Zondervan Publishing House edition 1950, 1952. Used by permission.

4. From *Unger's Bible Dictionary* by Merrill F. Unger (p. 208). Copyright © 1957, 1961, 1966. Moody Press. Moody Bible Institute of Chicago. Used by permission.

5. Lars Wilhelmsson, *Making Forever Friends* (Torrance, CA: The Martin Press, 1982), 112–113. Used by permission.

Chapter 9. Some Things Have Gotta Go!

1. Taken from *Fearfully and Wonderfully Made* by Paul Brand, M.D., with Philip Yancey (p. 20). Copyright © 1980 by Dr. Paul Brand and Philip Yancey. Used by permission of Zondervan Publishing House.

2. From Bruce Larson, *There's a Lot More to Health Than Not Being Sick,* copyright © 1981, p. 104; used by permission of Word Books, Publisher, Waco, Texas 76796.

Chapter 10. Choose for Yourself

1. Emma Lazarus, "The New Colossus."

2. From *Happiness Is a Choice* by Frank B. Minirth and Paul Meier. Copyright 1978 by Baker Book House and used by permission.

Chapter 11. The Necessity of Accountability

1. David Ansen, "Golden Boy of the Movies," *Newsweek,* 30 Nov. 1981, 106.

2. *Up with Worship* by Anne Ortlund (revised edition 1982, p. 102). © Copyright 1975, Regal Books, Ventura, CA 93006. Used by permission.

3. From Bruce Larson, *There's a Lot More to Health Than Not Being Sick,* copyright © 1981, p. 61; used by permission of Word Books, Publisher, Waco, Texas 76796.

Chapter 12. A Hope Transplant: The Essential Operation

1. Samuel Stevenson, "Where Is God's Power?" from *Poems That Preach,* compiled by John R. Rice (Wheaton, IL: Sword of the Lord Publishers, 1952), 78. Used by permission from The Sword of the Lord.

2. C. Neil Strait, *Quote Unquote,* compiled by Lloyd Cory (Wheaton, IL: Victor Books, A Division of SP Publications, Inc., 1977), 156. Used by permission.

3. Douglas Colligan, "That Helpless Feeling: The Dangers of Stress," *New York,* 14 July 1975, 30, 31.

4. Philip Yancey, *Where Is God When It Hurts?* (Grand Rapids, MI: Zondervan Publishing House, 1977), 142.

5. Carl Jung, quoted in M. Scott Peck, M.D., *The Road Less Traveled* (New York: Touchstone, Simon and Schuster, 1978). From *Collected Works of C. G. Jung,* Bollingen, Ser., No. 20, 2d ed. (Princeton, NJ: Princeton Univ. Press, 1973) trans. R. F. C. Hull, Vol. II, *Psychology and Religion: West and East,* 75.

6. M. Scott Peck, M.D., *The Road Less Traveled* (New York: Touchstone, Simon and Schuster, 1978), 16–17. Copyright © 1978 by M. Scott Peck, M.D. Reprinted by permission of Simon and Schuster, Inc.

Conclusion

1. Jordan Paul, Ph.D., and Margaret Paul, Ph.D., *Do I Have to Give Up Me to Be Loved By You?* (Minneapolis, MN: Comp-Care Publications, 1983), 165. Used by permission.

Other Word Products by Charles R. Swindoll

BIBLE STUDY GUIDES

A Ministry Anyone Could Trust
  (II Corinthians)
A Ministry Everyone Would
  Respect (II Corinthians)
Abraham
Beholding Christ, The Lamb of
  God (John 15–21)
Calm Answers, I Corinthians
Christ's Agony and Ecstasy
Coming to Terms with Sin
Contagious Christianity
Daniel
David
Dropping Your Guard
Exalting Christ, The Son of God
  (John 1–5)
Following Christ, The Man of
  God (John 6–14)
Galatians: Letter of Liberation
Growing Pains
Growing Up in God's Family
Hand Me Another Brick
Improving Your Serve
Issues and Answers
  (formerly Questions Christians
  Ask)

Jesus, Our Lord
Joseph: From Pit to Pinacle
Koinonia
Lamentations of Jeremiah
Learning to Walk by Grace
Letters to Churches
Living on the Ragged Edge
Moses
Living Above the Level of
  Mediocrity
New Testament Postcards
Old Testament Characters
Practical Helps, I Corinthians
Practical Life of Faith
Preeminent Person of Christ
Prophecy
Questions Christians Ask
Relating to Others in Love
Solomon
Spiritual Gifts
Steadfast Christianity
Stones of Remembrance
Strengthening Your Grip
Strong Reproofs, I Corinthians
You and Your Child
You and Your Problems

BOOKTRAX (Books on Cassette)

Improving Your Serve
Living Above the Level of Mediocrity
Living Beyond the Daily Grind, Book 1
Living Beyond the Daily Grind, Book 2
Living on the Ragged Edge
Strengthening Your Grip

VIDEO AND FILMS

People of Refuge. This single film provides practical examples for the church to become genuinely compassionate and friendly to the lonely and distress. Available on video cassette and 16mm film.

Strengthening Your Grip. Six powerful films that speak to all Christians about making the right choices, living adventurously, enjoying leisure without guilt, taking true godliness seriously, overcoming negative thinking, and establishing a biblical attitude toward authority. Available on video cassette and 16mm film.